D1015755

POLITICS
AND
PRACTICES
OF

INTERGOVERNMENTAL
EVALUATION

Comparative Policy Analysis Series
Ray C. Rist, Series Editor

Program Evaluation and the Management of Government,
edited by Ray C. Rist

Budgeting, Auditing, and Evaluation,
edited by Andrew Gray, Bill Jenkins, and Bob Segsworth

Can Governments Learn?
edited by Frans L. Leeuw, Ray C. Rist, and Richard C. Sonnichsen

Politics and Practices of Intergovernmental Evaluation,
edited by Olaf Rieper and Jacques Toulemonde

POLITICS

AND

PRACTICES

OF

INTERGOVERNMENTAL EVALUATION

OLAF RIEPER

AND

JACQUES TOULEMONDE

EDITORS

WITH A FOREWORD BY
RAY C. RIST

TRANSACTION PUBLISHERS
New Brunswick (U.S.A.) and London (U.K.)

Library of Congress Catalog Number: 96-30780
ISBN: 1-56000-256-5
Printed in the United States of America

Library of Congress Cataloging-in-Publication Data

Politics and practices of intergovernmental evaluation / edited by Olaf Rieper and Jacques Toulemonde ; with a foreword by Ray C. Rist.
    p. cm. — (Comparative policy analysis series)
Includes bibliographical references and index.
ISBN 1-56000-256-5 (alk. paper)
    1. Central-local government relations—Evaluation. 2. Federal government—Evaluation. 3. Political planning—Evaluation. I. Rieper, Olaf. II. Toulemonde, Jacques. III. Series.
JS113.P64   1996
351.09'3—dc20
                                     96-30780
                                         CIP

Contents

Foreword

One of the challenging and intriguing difficulties of research is to recognize that which is right in front of you. The research impulse is to seek out the nuances, the idiosyncratic, and the obscure. The self-evident is ignored.

This difficulty has not escaped the evaluation community. Great intellectual effort has gone into the development of sophisticated designs and methodologies for the study of individual policies, programs, and projects. Costly efforts to find the smallest evidence of a policy or program impact are undertaken in the presumption that such data are central to policy decision making. The emphasis has been overwhelmingly to find discrete impacts from discrete governmental initiatives. Indeed, in the United States, the most frequently used term when discussing evaluation is to refer to "program" evaluation, that is, the study of an individual initiative or activity.

What has been ignored in the evaluation community is the fact of the intergovernmental nature of political and policy governance—regardless of which specific nation state one might choose. Whether it is Canada, the United States, England, Denmark, Sweden, Germany, Japan, or any other of the industrial countries, the governmental structure is essentially a web of interrelated policies, programs, and projects. The political mosaic has both vertical and horizonal components, but it is, indeed, a mosaic. Understanding local responsibilities and requirements for funding housing construction, for example, necessitates also an understanding of the role that regional and national governmental agencies and administrations also play in the scheme of housing. The same can be said for transportation, energy, health care, telecommunications, and on and on.

The point, quite simply, is that governance in complex democratic societies necessitates the coordination and cooperation of multiple levels of government. Sometimes, there is duplication and overlapping levels of jurisdiction, at other times it is more neat. But the totality of governing agencies at whatever level are woven together into a political system. It is the nature of this system that it is inherently intergovernmental. There are areas where one level of government has most if not sole responsibility for a governance function, but these are noteworthy by their being the exception. In their totality, democratic systems embrace local, regional, and national levels of governance; they embrace multiple sectors of public activity and responsibility; and authority to act is portioned out via an intricate set of regulations, laws, judicial rulings, and constitutional requirements.

If the above is at all accurate as a quick sketch of the system of governance in democratic political systems, then the appearance of this volume, *The Policy and Practice of Intergovernmental Evaluation*, merits special attention. It does so for two reasons, each of which would by itself be sufficient justification for the publication. Taken together, this book becomes both the benchmark and landmark for work in the area of the evaluation of intergovernmental policies, programs, and projects.

First, it has taken on directly the issue of intergovernmental evaluation, a topic that seems to have illuded the attention of the evaluation community for the past thirty years. Major textbooks in the field do not address the topic. It is not, for example, listed in the index of either Rossi and Freeman's opus, *Evaluation* (5th edition) or in the index to Patton's volume, *Qualitative Evaluation and Research Methods* (2nd edition). Further, and this is most telling, it is not listed as one of the topics or concepts discussed by Michael Scriven in his recently published, *Evaluation Thesaurus*, a more than 400-page treatment of the key terms in evaluation.

The irony of this should not be lost. Evaluation has grown and matured as a response to the needs of the public sector in general and the policymaking community in particular. What appears to have emerged over these past decades is a situation where the policy community did not ask and the evaluation community did not offer. Both may intrinsically have well understood the difficultly in moving into intergovernmental issues. The policy community has had reason to shy away for in this realm, accountability is diffuse and fractured, the demands for coordination and cooperation are large, and the evidence of successful outcomes and impacts are hard to demonstrate—as the chapters in this present book make clear. Further, it is hard for any individual politician or policy maker to take much credit for what outcomes are achieved. The diffusion of responsibility across levels of government and across multiple actors in the policy arena means any claim to fame is hard to make. From their vantage point in making the political calculations, there are too many players and too little visibility.

The evaluation community has also not stepped forward to take the lead in this area. Intergovernmental programs make for a most difficult set of circumstances for evaluators. To wit: there are often diffuse sets of goals at different levels of government (quite deliberately done to ensure the acceptance of the initiative at the different levels—allowing each level to interpret the intentions to their own advantage); there are different sets of players who have different sets of expectations for the policy or program and will define success in their own terms; the data systems are not aligned across levels of government to ensure some degree of consistency in measurement and tracking of performance; and the range of stakeholders can vary so considerably at different governmental levels that achieving consensus on the goals and objectives of the evaluation itself will inevitably be difficult and maybe impossible. In the face of these circumstances, the evaluators quietly slip back into the comfortable environs of studying individual policies, programs, or projects, and turn away from the complexity of the intergovernmental system.

The second major contribution of this volume lies in it being comparative and cross-national in its perspective and content. No other such book exists on this topic. The material presented here not only provides a systematic theoretical and empirical treatment of intergovernmental evaluation, but does so with case material from seven nations and the European Union. The materials range from the study of individual cantons and their relation to the Swiss government across a range of topics to the manner in which the European Union is now driving more and more of the regional and national policy agendas of the member states. Indeed, the emergence of the European Union as a powerful political force in Europe is directly affecting the development of evaluation as a craft. Questions are now being asked and levels of expertise are being expected across Europe that did not exist even a scant five years ago.

The strengths of this comparative approach are several. The comparative perspective reinforces the intellectual vitality and robustness of the concept of intergovernmental evaluation. The fact that it is not much discussed does not mean it is not present nor important. Many important issues in the policy arena go largely undiscussed. Further, it is a concept that clearly holds across different nation states with different political and policy configurations.

The comparative perspective also brings into sharp relief the manner in which governments have chosen to organize themselves and along what dimensions in different countries one finds similarities and contrasts. Understanding how, for example, Switzerland and Sweden each organize their intergovernmental systems brings clarity to an understanding of each in comparison to the other. The same would hold true in the instances of Canada and the United States. Indeed, the comparisons need not be in matched pairs. The framework in this book allows one to look across a number of countries on any given dimension and see how each country responds to that particular aspect of governance and how they seek to know of the performance of that dimension via evaluation.

Further, it is in the context of deciding how to evaluate such intergovernmental programs within the different countries that the evaluator has to know the organizational logic of the government. Effective intergovernmental evaluation cannot occur when the evaluator is working with blinders firmly in place, focusing on just the individual policy, program, or project. As noted above, they are webbed into the policy structure of the country. It is this understanding of the web that becomes so crucial to grasping the nature of the intergovernmental relationships.

The editors and contributors to this volume are to be commended for their efforts to bring into sharp relief the central role that intergovernmental relations play in the governance of democratic societies. Further, they have taken us into the uncharted waters of how we might evaluate such relations. That they have done so with such clarity and conviction that intergovernmental evaluation is central to the governance of our societies deserves both our attention and our thanks.

Ray C. Rist
Washington, D.C.

Introduction:
Politics and Practice of
Intergovernmental Evaluation

Jacques Toulemonde and Olaf Rieper

Intergovernmental Evaluation is an Unknown Land

In almost all countries and policy domains, governments interact in designing, financing, or implementing their programs. This book attempts to demonstrate how these same governments also interact when the time has come to evaluate these programs. The focus here is on how evaluations may be decided, designed, managed, and utilized within an intergovernmental system.

The presumption here is that intergovernmental evaluation (IGE) is of critical interest, and can be meaningfully distinguished from other kinds of evaluation. The reasons why serious attention must be paid to IGE lie in the extensive development of joint policies and programs by multiple levels of government, a trend which is much more pervasive than the reading of constitutions and laws suggest. Consider the following examples.

A look at the federal system in the United States reveals several thousand intergovernmental programs. Lobbyists employed by business firms, labor unions, and citizen groups and the employees of national, state, and local governments constantly cross each other's paths to influence decisions at all levels. The U.S. federal system is ideally seen as a layer cake, but the marble cake is now the standard analogy (Sharkanski, 1981).

In Germany, another federal system, the exercise of most governing functions is shared between the federal government and the *Länder.* These common tasks are of growing importance despite the fact that the constitution establishes rigorous separations between the different levels (Scharpf, 1988).

1

In the French unitary system, the hierarchic model has exploded in the last few decades. This results both from the setting up of the European Union and from the emergence of autonomous regional and local powers. The new levels of government were initially thought of as having independent fields of jurisdiction. In practice, the instances of overlapping are so frequent that intergovernmental policies are becoming the rule. In some extreme but not exceptional cases, European programs involve no less than five levels of government before producing their output on the French territory.

In the smaller, unitary Nordic countries various distinct levels of government have been in existence for more than half a century: the municipalities, the counties and the national governments. Each level has its own elected body of governance and its specific tasks. However, especially during the last decades, national policies have been crossing through the various levels, reflecting a high degree of inter-level dependency.

These examples confirm that many policies and programs involve several levels of government (federations, states, regions, municipalities) and that the sharing of responsibilities between levels is often far from stabilized. Consequently, we should expect to find a number of evaluations which intend to assess joint policies and programs or which aim at justifying new shifts or drifts in the borders of policy fields. But do such evaluations exist? Are they carried out in a manner that reflects the intergovernmental nature of the program? Do they pose specific problems?

Trying to answer these question requires an initial definition of intergovernmental. We propose the following: an evaluation is intergovernmental if two levels of government interact during at least one stage of the evaluation process, the first stage being the decision to evaluate and the final one being the utilization of evaluation findings.

Although our definition is relatively broad, we are surprised to observe that there are very few IGEs in comparison with the worldwide growth of intricate intergovernmental relations. This unbalance seems to be reflected in the available literature. There are many good books and papers on intergovernmental relations, despite Rhodes' (1981) complaint about major remaining defects, but the literature on intergovernmental evaluation is almost nonexistent.

Reasons must be sought for this paradoxical imbalance. IGE obviously faces specific political, organizational, and technical difficulties that will be analyzed in this book and that explain the paradox in part.

However, in a perfect world where all practical difficulties would be overcome, the unbalance might remain, due to the fact that "single-government evaluations" may happen to be the best choice when dealing with joint policies and programs.

Whatever the reasons that make research on IGE so scarce, the authors are convinced that a domain which appears to be unknown territory is worth exploring. However, one cannot progress in new directions with the same means as in secure fields. This explains some of the book's special features: (1) it starts by taking its bearings firmly and by equipping itself with a set of precise definitions; (2) it gives the authors freedom to explore many different intergovernmental situations, with a deliberate choice in favor of overviewing the whole area in an heuristic way rather than applying a rigorous comparative method; (3) it does not conclude with robust research-based findings, but by marking out new territories.

Before briefly introducing each of the following chapters it should be stressed that the book represents an integrated whole despite the variations in policies, programs, and political contexts. The authors' ambition is to take the reader on a tour through the landscape of evaluations which has only one predefined aspect, namely their intergovernmental character. In doing so the reader is invited to reflect on each of the national contributions addressing a common set of questions. These questions concern challenges for those who order evaluations as well for those who design and implement evaluations. Some of the questions are framed as hypotheses and expectations, which are dealt with in the following chapters.

One set of challenges is supposed to stem from the very fact that characterizes levels of government, namely that each level of government has its own electorate, its own legitimacy, and therefore potentially has heavily vested interests in the evaluation of a programme, which might differ from those of other levels of government. This introduces a special problem for the evaluator in serving many masters. Obviously a huge and complex pattern of factors influence the surfacing of tension due to accountability to various electorates.

One might expect the political and administrative climate surrounding the program and its evaluation to be of importance. Is the evaluation dealing with very sensitive politcal questions in an adverse climate, or with routine problems in a consensual climate? Or is it to be expected, that across variations of political climate the type of relations between the levels of government, which are involved in the evaluation process, somehow influence the surfacing of the potential conflict? Does a bilateral relation between government raise more diversity in views than a relation where only one level of government takes the lead? Or in situations where the levels of government do not interact at all? In the next section different types of relations are described.

Thus, in reading the national contributions the reader might ask: Under what circumstances do divergent views develop? Do they materialize in situations where the levels of government have a bilateral and partnership relation to each other? Or also in situations where one level of government is leading the evaluation?

But, however, if conflict is near the surface, how does one cope with it in a more technical sense? By focusing the evaluation to avoid sensitive questions? By narrowing the evaluation questions? By focusing the evaluation on intermediary goals in order to avoid divergent views on outcome in relation to ultimate goals?

The reader is urged to reflect on whether the above challenges of IGE might meaningfully be dealt with in only a technical sense. Does the pressure from different political constituencies of different levels of government make an evaluation relevant to all levels of government almost impossible? And is this the explanation of why so few IGEs are described in the literature in a period where the number of intergovernmental programs explodes?

Another, though related, set of questions concerns the issue of the utilization of IGE. From the challenges mentioned above it is obvious that the tension rooted in the very nature of intergovernmental relations might prevent utilization by more than one level of government or prevent any utilization at all. Following the typology from the literature on the use of evaluation the reader might identify various models of utilization, and ask how the nature of intergovernmental relations hinders or furthers utilization. Does use according to the managerial model become constrained by technical reasons, such as distance from the field data, and difficulties in synthesizing information across levels of government? Is democratic use by politicians and the public restrained by the very nature of IGE, putting the levels of government into competition or even conflict over the evaluation findings? Does a model of shared conceptual use imply a learning feed back loop, become relevant in situations where interlevel consensus is relatively high, and where a policy and professional community exists?

Is it meaningful to distinguish between the different models of use when confronted with the realities of IGE? Is the most promising way to enhance use by securing the closest possible interaction between levels of government?

These are some of the major questions and challenges we believe IGE raises for administrators and politicians ordering evaluations, for those who design and conduct evaluations in an intergovernmental way, and for the researchers dealing with evaluation systems. Trace these issues, and others you may want to raise, during your guided IGE tour through various western countries. The empirical richness of the national chapters will make it worthwhile.

Origins and Content of a Collective Book

This book, and especially this introductory chapter, deals with definitions and tries to identify potentially fruitful paths of research. It is the result of tough and difficult debates that took place over three years within the IIAS Working Group on Policy and Program Evaluation. Chapters 2 to 8 are national contributions.

In our basic set of examples, two cases dealt with the European Community (Rieper and Toulemonde) and one with federal/provincial interaction in Canada. Only the Swedish case was related to a unitary state. For this reason, we made several attempts to add at least one chapter emanating from a centralized state. With this purpose in mind, contacts were made in both France and England and we were very glad that Mary Henkel finally accepted to join our project as she has a long and well-known record of research on topics close to intergovernmental evaluation.

In the light of the striking changes that occurred in the U.S. evaluation landscape in the 1980s, we obviously needed to include an American chapter. In what way was evaluation affected by the decentralization impulse during the Reagan years? Did this lead to more evaluation at state level or to joint evaluation at federal and state level? Linda Morra has accepted to answer these important questions with the authority bestowed on her by the GAO, although she naturally speaks on her own behalf.

Although we finally conclude that distinguishing federal and unitary states does not really make a difference in intergovernmental evaluation, we initially thought that more input should come from federal systems. For this reason we made several requests in the direction of Germany and Australia. Finally an answer came from Switzerland, not so big a country nor a continent ! But one must realize how much Switzerland, given its exotic constitutional system, is interesting with respect to interaction between levels of government. The Swiss case, together with that of the European Union, provides us with the most decentralized example of policymaking. We are grateful to Willy Zimermann and Peter Knoepfel for shedding light on a small territory which may help us to a better understanding of large areas of our problem.

The reader has probably realized that the final set of national chapters result more from opportunity than from the rational ruminations of the editors. This could not be avoided in a project which exclusively depended on the goodwill of volunteers. When we consider that it has been possible to study intergovernmental evaluation in such a variety of different situations, we finally think that good fortune must have presided in the process which has led to the following national chapters :

Jan Eric Furubo, from the Swedish National Court of Audit and from the European Evaluation Society, presents a systematic study of intergovernmental relations in the field of education in his country. His chapter focuses on interaction between the national and municipality levels. It presents a very curious and interesting situation where decentralization leads to decreasing interaction, while evaluation seems to concentrate on the remaining intergovernmental relations.

Mary Henkel, from Brunel University, United Kingdom, draws a portrait of evaluation in her country with examples from the fields of social services and education. She focuses on interaction between national and regional levels of government. Her chapter highlights the transmission of evaluation culture from higher to lower levels through a series of processes initially designed for control. Common evaluation culture may constitute as critical a component for IGE as, for example, common goal clarification, common data collection, or common utilization of results.

Linda Morra, from the United States General Accounting Office, summarizes the history of the separate development of evaluation at federal and state levels. Her examples mainly relate to the fields of education and training programs. She illustrates the hypothesis that is the basis of this book and that can be expressed as follows: strong interaction between governments on policy fields and jointly implemented programs do not automatically lead to intergovernmental evaluation.

In their joint chapter *Dale Poel and Robert Segsworth*, from, respectively, the Dalhousie and Laurentian Universities in Canada, present an interesting and rigorous comparison between two IGE cases studies: one in the field of employment and the other in the field of justice. They focus on interaction between federal and provincial levels. Both examples involve strong interaction on policy fields, but the two evaluations take very different forms, one being carried out with a research design that reflects the intergovernmental character of the program and the other unilaterally.

Olaf Rieper, from the Institute of Local Governments Studies in Denmark, has developed an in-depth case study in the field of regional development policy. His chapter involves no less than four levels of government, encompassing Europe, national government, county and municipalities. The program under evaluation results from an intricate sharing of responsibilities between levels. Evaluation itself is formally organized in an intergovernmental fashion. This chapter perhaps shows the situation which is closest to an ideal IGE. As such, it highlights the problems that arise as a result of a multilevel evaluation and suggests ways of solving them.

Jacques Toulemonde, from the ENTPE in France and from Centre for European Evaluation Expertise, presents an overview of evaluation practice within the European Commission, with examples taken in regional policy and R&D policy. He focuses on interaction between European and Member State levels. Various situations are studied, from the strongest to the weakest intergovernmental policies and evaluations. When looking at an environment where the sharing of responsibilities is subject to permanent debates between levels, it appears that some evaluations serve as arguments or even as weapons in the battle for redefining policy borders.

Willy Zimmermann and Peter Knoepfel, respectively from the Universities of Geneva and Lausanne, Switzerland, report on an evaluation they carried out in the field of environment policy. Their work involved confederate and cantonal levels with strong interaction evident for both the policy and its evaluation. This chapter suggests that vertical separations between policy networks, between professional groups or between lobbies may sometimes make more sense than horizontal limits between levels of government.

The final chapter faces the difficult task of synthesizing a deliberately heterogeneous series of contributions. Since the book's exploratory character must be admitted, it cannot claim to draw robust conclusions from a comparison of research materials collected. The most which can be done is to sketch a sort of geographic map of this rather unknown land whose name is intergovernmental evaluation.

Governments Have Autonomous Political Resources

What are the basic features which distinguish a government from the other type of organizations involved in public activities? Due to the ups and downs of decentralization, the growing trend towards contracting out and the continuing role played by semi-state bodies, it is often difficult to distinguish governments from quasi-governmental organizations, agencies, or mere layers of administration.

Rhodes (1981) suggests that the very nature of a government must be sought in its political autonomy. More precisely, he speaks of discretion in the use of power resources. These power resources are of a various nature: a government may or may not have its own constitutional independence, its own legitimacy, its own political life with specific democratic arenas, its own system of checks and balances, its own public opinion, its own political elites, its own tax-raising power, its own budget, its own administrative skills and expertise, its own information system, its own procedures and controls, and so on. Note that certain power resources are similar in all organizations, governmental or not, for example: budget, control and information. But other resources which belong to the political sphere are specific to governments, for example: legitimacy, public opinion, checks and balances.

Only fully independent democratic nations have governments which enjoy total autonomy in the use of the full range of power resources. If complete autonomy were the critical criterion, it is difficult to accept that provinces, regions, counties or municipalities have governments. But for the purpose of this book, it is more appropriate to speak of relative autonomy and to use Rhodes' criteria for diagnosing how close the institutions under study are to the absolute definition of a government. Obviously, an institution that has no discretion in the use of political power resources is not a government. We believe that this restriction applies to organizations like universities, hospitals and agencies which we do not consider to be subject matter for this book.

Any government is, or should be, accountable to its own electorate. Within a single level of government, these electorates are in juxtaposition. Constituencies are independent of one another and do not overlap from a geographic point of view. No voter may simultaneously belong to several areas of authority of the same level.

A conceptual problem arises when several governments of the same level decide to cooperate and set up common procedures and institutions for this purpose. In this case, their common group does not constitute a separate level of government as long as its political legitimacy comes from the founding governments. According to our definition, a new level only appears when the cooperation group gains some kind of direct political legitimacy without the intervention of its founding governments.

Consequently, we consider that the powerful associations of local authorities in the Nordic countries belong to the local level, because their democratic basis is local, even if they enjoy political visibility at the national level.

The case of the European Union is less clear since most of the power belongs to the member states although some elements of autonomous political legitimacy do exist at the European level. The European Council of Heads of States and Governments can be viewed as belonging to the national level, especially when it decides under the rule of unanimity. But the same institution may appear to belong to the European level in other circumstances. Once again, the definition turns out to be a question of degree rather than one of clear-cut distinctions.

A common problem arises from the fact that upper levels of government often have to implement their policies at street level. This means allocating money to individual beneficiaries and applying regulations to local citizens, local companies or local groups. This is the policy law of gravity described as follows: "the buck drops down to local officials at street level." The public money and regulations may reach the local level either directly or through intermediary levels of government. If it is via this latter route, one can conceive of a policy fountain with funds cascading down between levels.

At any level of government full responsibility for a policy or program does not automatically mean direct central administration. In fact, there are three ways of implementing a single-government policy: direct central administration, direct decentral administration and indirect administration.

Direct central administration is the simplest scheme. It means that the officials at one level of government are able to implement the policy themselves. They play the role of the "street-level bureaucracy." The European Competition Policy is an example in point: about forty European officials control the merging of enterprises throughout Europe. They are mainly involved in high-level contacts with multinational firms. This example shows that upper levels can efficiently implement a policy on their own, provided the main stakeholders operate at the same territorial level. Nevertheless, direct central administration is generally more suited to the lower levels of government, these being closer to street level.

Direct decentral administration is often used when the government is too distant from its target and equips itself with a street-level layer of administration. The street level layer reports to the central government and the system involves guidelines and controls enabling the central government to maintain full responsibility for the policy. There are plenty of examples of policies which operate through local layers of administration: the FBI in the U.S., the French education system, and the labor laws in Denmark, to name three.

Indirect administration occurs when a government has its policy implemented by controlled tiers: agencies, trusts, non-profit making associations, or private firms. Control is exerted either through contracting out a specific task or through a representative who sits on the board of directors.

An example of indirect administration is that of the network linking the 217 local action groups involved in the E.U. Leader program which aims at promoting rural development through supporting innovative local development. The European network is managed by a Belgian non-profit making association selected after a call for tenders.

Intergovernmental Policies Imply Sharing Responsibility

In the case of intergovernmental relations, the tasks of designing, implementing and/or evaluating are shared between different levels of government. Since each level of government is normally independent of the others, their shared responsibility raises specific problems. For example, when different levels of governments are accountable to different electorates, each level may have legitimate but contradictory goals. Thus, shared responsibility has dramatic consequences on major evaluative questions like the clarification of goals, the assessment of effectiveness, or specification as to who is accountable. Since the evaluation patterns are likely to be different in a context of shared responsibility, a clear border must be drawn between full and shared responsibility. Special attention must be paid to the risk of confusing layers of administration, those with full responsibility, and those with shared responsibility.

Intergovernmental relations may digress from partnership and co-operation to competition and open conflict. Competing policies run by different levels of government are sometimes targeted at very similar groups or have closely related objectives. In this case, evaluations may become involved in intergovernmental competition or may even be used as a weapon in the fight for power between levels.

Wright (1978) considers that policy areas may be shaped in three ways: (1) the separated model where levels are functionally autonomous and develop few relations; (2) the overlapping model where the main form of relation is bargaining; and (3) the inclusive model where relations are organized in a hierarchic way. Of course, intergovernmental questions are mainly drawn from the overlapping model. Worldwide observation shows that this model is frequent. It does not only apply to federal or confederal systems but also to unitary states.

To consider that a single intergovernmental scheme applies to the totality of a given political system would be a clear case of oversimplification. In fact, a constitutional landscape often includes different areas where one or another of the three models applies. For example, different policy fields such as education, health or technology may be either separated, overlapping or inclusive. Different stages of the policy process may also follow different models: policy design and implementation may overlap while evaluation is separated or vice-versa. Finally, changing models can apply to the same policy area at different points in time, a hierarchic policy becoming more and more overlapping.

Intergovernmental Relations Involve
Symmetry of Power Resources

Dependence in intergovernmental systems is a two-way street and must be conceived from the very beginning as belonging to a symmetry of powers. Each level has discretionary use of certain power resources and depends on its counterpart for other resources. According to Rhodes (1981), interaction between levels can follow three different models: the agent model, the cooperative model and the intergovernmental model which is the only one applicable here.

In the agent model, upper level policymakers are free to organize their policy (or program). They can easily reshape the methods of designing, implementing and/or evaluating their policy. They can withdraw responsibility from local governments and contract the job out to agencies, trusts, or private firms. They can also choose direct management. Even if several levels of government are involved, the balance of power is clearly in favor of the upper level which can design and redesign the inter-organizational structure. Local levels implement the policies of the upper levels under a supervision system which may include financial dependence and detailed controls. When public organizations interact in such a dissymmetric form, the lower level does not play the role of a government but rather that of a layer of administration or an agency.

In the cooperative model, different area authorities at the lower level decide to undertake collectively a strictly delimited policy. This takes the shape akin to a joint diplomatic agreement into which area authorities feel free to enter or not. No government is developed at the upper level and the balance of power is definitely in favor of the lower level. This is typically the case of many international agencies in their relation to national states, but the model can also apply to lower levels. For example, when neighboring municipalities set up a co-operative body to implement common public investments, they face diplomatic problems which are basically comparable to those of governments running an international agency.

In the intergovernmental model, each level relies on its counterpart(s) to design, to implement and/or to evaluate a common policy. Levels are equals according to constitutional rules and each has discretionary use of one or more key resources. They are interdependent in a symmetric way. It is difficult to tilt the intergovernmental relation because no level has the power to reshape the powers of the other levels.

Restricting the Study to the Basic Interaction Across Two Levels

At first glance, it appears plausible to categorize intergovernmental relations into the three traditional forms of constitutions: federal, confederal, and unitary. We have already illustrated that the reality is much more complicated.

In any constitutional system, intergovernmental relations are heterogeneous, each policy area having its own distinctive characteristics. The architecture of intergovernmental relations is not only complex, it is also dynamic. Some authors have seen a worldwide drift to stronger governments at the higher levels, which is obviously the trend in the American federalism (Sharkanski, 1981) and in the European Community. However, the opposite can be observed in Canada, Spain, Belgium, France, Italy, and in Nordic countries. Meanwhile, countries like Great Britain and Germany have experienced successive periods of relaxed and increased pressure by one level upon another. Considering such opposite trends, Rhodes (1981) thinks that federalism and decentralization have become virtually synonymous.

How to Work Out a Comparative Study in a Disparate and Changing World?

We think that no full comparison can be made between such highly complex systems as Western democracies. Thus, to enable some limited comparisons, we have chosen to proceed with a focus on a simple comparable unit: interaction between two neighboring levels of government. The rationale for the synthesis with which this book ends, lies in the hypothesis that a few common rules apply to the basic relation between two levels of government whatever the country, the constitutional system, the policy field and the "altitude" above street level.

We accept that such an hypothesis may be too restrictive in some cases. For example, when three, four, or five levels of government are related to one another, our reasoning might not cover specific intergovernmental relations of which a typical case is the bypass occurring when a level of government attempts to create direct links with a level which is not its closest neighbor. This is an excellent way to gain power in intergovernmental relations and this game is played by the European Commission and the regions in a way which is unwelcome to the member states. Nevertheless, we think it is worth concentrating on the dual intergovernmental relationship, with findings which are generally applicable, instead of describing curious intergovernmental configurations much like a butterfly collector.

Unified Interaction or Diversely Shaped Relations

However welcome any relevant simplification may be, we cannot avoid looking more closely at the role of the lower level. Since this level is inevitably made up of several area authorities, there is a natural trend for intergovernmental relations to take a differentiated shape according to the different governments which operate at the lower level. The following paragraphs present three shapes of interaction which lead either to unified or to diverse intergovernmental relations.

In the first model of bilateral interaction, activities are not entirely shaped by the upper level, but a special negotiation takes place between the upper level and each of the area authorities at the lower level. Negotiations with different governments at the lower level produce different packages of activities, different systems of implementation, and even give birth to different goals or different evaluation criteria. These differences do not only result from the process of conducting parallel negotiations, but also from the fact that the different area authorities at the lower level do not have an equal bargaining power or similar social needs.

It is difficult to find pure examples of such bilateral interactions since every policy or program invariably has a common unified core. But two European examples are not very far from this theoretical model: (1) the French *Contrats de Plan Etat-Région* which organize an intergovernmental framework of public investments through separate negotiations between the central state and each of the twenty-six regions, and (2) the European Community Support Frameworks which result from separate negotiations between the European Community and each member state and lead to distinctive regional policies throughout Europe.

In the second model, interaction is shaped in a standard way at the upper level. Area authorities at the lower levels mainly exert their power through their decision in favor or against the interaction. Of course, having decided to interact, the lower level can develop the whole range of manoeuvres which is always attached to autonomous actors but which is not specific to intergovernmental relations. Numerous cases of such relationships can be found in almost all countries. For example, the Job Training Partnership Act in the U.S. was designed, funded, and evaluated in a unified way at the federal level. States that chose to be involved at implementation and evaluation stages were not allowed to significantly re-shape the federal frameworks.

In the third model, interaction takes place through a single negotiation process that includes the upper level and all the area authorities at the lower level (either directly or indirectly through their representatives). A good example of triangular relationship is the German regional policy (*Gemeinschaftsaufsgabe*) which was designed, monitored, and evaluated under the control of a joint council, of which half the members were representatives of the *Länder*, the other half of the federal level. An other example from a unitary state is the role played by the municipalities in Nordic countries vis-à-vis the national government. The national association of local governments in each country negotiates with various sections of the national government on behalf of all the lower level area authorities. These negotiations end up as genuine treaties between levels of government.

Intergovernmental Evaluation

For the purpose of international comparison the studies presented in this book encompass more than the evaluation of programs. Public management through programs is a somewhat marginal practice in certain countries. We speak more generally of policy evaluation which also includes schemes, laws, contracts, measures, as well as programs.

For the same reasons, we speak of ex-post facto and ongoing evaluation or more generally, of any attempt to judge a policy through a specifically designed collection of field data.

In the same spirit of generalization we allow our studies to encompass the whole scope of evaluation questions: effectiveness, efficiency, coherence, relevance, utility and all goals: measurement, understanding, judgment, and negotiation.

Although our view of evaluation encompasses a lot of different practices, it still fits definitions which are commonly accepted like that of Rist (1989): "Evaluation is the application of systematic research methods to the assessment of policy and program design, implementation and effectiveness."

According to Simeon (1972), an intergovernmental policy is made by independent actors at different levels, who belong to a common social and institutional environment, who share some goals, who negotiate on a set of issues in a nonhierarchical way, who use varying power resources in a strategic and tactical way and finally, who produce common outcomes with consequences for themselves, for others and for the whole system. We do not restrict ourselves to the policies which correspond to this definition. We think that a policy can be intergovernmental at the design stage, at the implementation stage, at the evaluation stage, or at one or more of these stages.

This is why it may be helpful to draw an intergovernmental profile of the specific policy under evaluation. This profile should include, at the very least, the following items:

- Design stage
    1. At which level is the legal framework designed? Are the domains of jurisdiction clearly defined and allocated to different levels?
    2. At which level is the political agenda fixed? Are the dates and deadlines of both levels the same?
    3. Are there discrepancies in the beneficiary areas?
    4. Which model does the decision-making process follow (agent, cooperative, intergovernmental)? Is the policy unified or diverse?
- Implementation stage
    5. Are there co-financed activities involving several different levels?
    6. Is there a common monitoring committee or any other system for jointly controlling the implementation stage?
    7. Is there a joint-information system?
- Evaluation stage
    8. Is there interaction between levels at the evaluation stage, or are there competing evaluations by both levels or a single evaluation by one level?

Figure 1.1 shows an example of a policy profile from the European Framework Program for Research and Development, which has been the subject of an evaluation in 1992, which was an intergovernmental evaluation involving the Member States and the European Commission.

Figure 1.2 gives a second example of an intergovernmental profile of an evaluation: the evaluation of the European "support framework" in Ireland which was undertaken jointly in 1989 by governments at two levels.

Figure 1.1
Intergovernmental Profile of the European Framework
Program for Research and Development

	Member States	Both	European Commission
Design			
Legal framework		x	
Agenda		x	
Decision		x	
Implementation			
Funding			x
Monitoring		x	
Evaluation		x	

Figure 1.2
Intergovernmental Profile of the 1989 Evaluation of the
European "Support Framework" in the Republic of Ireland

	Republic of Ireland	Both	European Commission
Which level?			
Sets up the legal framework		x	
Sets up the agenda			x
Launches the evaluation		x	
Pays for the evaluation			x
Words the questions		x	
Designs the method		x	
Collects and processes data	x		
Receives the draft report			x
Receives the final report		x	
Uses the findings		x	

Is Intergovernmental Evaluation Workable?

In an intergovernmental situation, several technical problems are likely to occur during an evaluation, such as the following.

1. Specific Problems in Collecting and Pooling Data

To a large extent, IGEs encounter the same difficulties as multisite evaluations. Multisite evaluations deal with programs that are implemented in a similar way over multiple sites. Literature on multisite evaluation tries to sort out and solve problems which arise when synthetic conclusions are to be based on decentralized research designs (Lobosco and Kaufman, 1989; Sinacore and Turpin, 1991).

Multiplying the sites of data collection may be a serious impediment to evaluation. The greater the number of lower level area authorities involved in the evaluation process, the more numerous are the gatekeepers who have to be convinced to give access to information and the more varied are the cultural barriers which have to be overcome. Alternatively, it may be worth involving numerous stakeholders at a lower level in the evaluation process as this may help to enhance utilization, strengthen validity, general scope, and credibility.

Evaluation staff may be hired and supervised either at the upper or lower level. In the latter case, special attention must be paid to training and coordinating local evaluators in order to set up a common framework for data collection (at least for the common core of data), and check the quality of data. Local evaluators may advocate local programs, especially if naturalistic methods are used since these encourage evaluators to immerse themselves in the local environment.

Data can be processed either at the upper or lower level. In the first case, field data are aggregated at the upper level (pooling by lumping). In the second case, the upper level works with data which have been already averaged at the lower level (pooling by averaging). Both methods give rise to specific problems which emerge from the evaluation design (inductive/deductive, quantitative/qualitative).

2. Specific Problems in Identifying and Sharing Outcomes

Outputs are produced at the point where the policy interacts with its target, whereas outcomes are produced at more distant stages of social processes. Outputs remain more or less in the policymakers' hands while outcomes clearly are not. This distinguishes the fields of management which deals with outputs as opposed to evaluation which deals with outcomes.

In the case of IGE, there is a specific difficulty in distinguishing outputs from outcomes, which may lead to confusing, misleading problems of method. For the upper level, outputs can be produced at the street level, where the policy reaches its target. But street-level interaction is beyond upper-level control and what happens at this stage should, in fact, be called outcomes. Viewed from the top, outputs should be the change in lower-level behavior due to upper-level policy. Thus, IGEs must systematically ask two evaluative questions: (1) Is the policy successful in changing the behavior of one or both levels of government? (2) Is the policy successful in changing the behavior of the target group?

The more additional levels of governments are involved in a policy, the more likely it is that evaluation will devote attention to the impacts on intermediary public bodies. This might lead to an evaluation practice focusing on bureaucratic and diplomatic processes at the expense of social outcomes. Is it possible to observe such a trend?

When two levels of government implement a shared policy, especially when they co-finance the policy in question, it is likely that evaluators will be required to cut the outcome cake into two parts, each part being a benefit resulting from one government's policy. They will be asked to address questions like: what is the value added by each level of government in terms of effectiveness of the policy, or alternatively, is the cost to each level appropriate to its benefits? It is widely recognized that few evaluators are successful in disentangling the complex network of causes and effects. Since they have to handle this additional design problem, intergovernmental evaluators face a hurdle generally more difficult than is found in single-level evaluation.

3. Specific Problems in Taking Contradictory Criteria into Account

A naive question must be asked: does the same evaluation method lead to the same conclusion if applied to different levels of government? The answer is clearly negative, as indicated by the following example. In the field of economic and social development policies, many British evaluations use cost-effectiveness logic and attempt to compute "cost per net job" ratios. Many evaluators agree that such evaluations must take into account the displacement effect: an additional job should not be attributed to a policy outcome if it results from the loss of an equivalent job elsewhere. But how is the term "elsewhere" defined—the rest of the beneficiary area, the rest of the UK or the rest of the EC? The result will obviously depend on the evaluator's standpoint and the political considerations of the stakeholders.

This means that the same method, applied on behalf of different levels of government, will produce different results. Similar examples of intergovernmental concerns can be observed in many evaluation techniques. In fact, they clarify a problem that is basically not a technical one. There is necessarily a rationale for a level of government to become involved in a policy field. Thus, it would not make sense if two interacting levels of government shared exactly the same rationale. If this were the case, one of the levels would not be able to justify its *raison d'être*. It is unlikely, therefore, that an IGE could produce common technical answers to evaluative questions posed from two different standpoints.

Is Intergovernmental Evaluation Relevant?

As we noted at the beginning of this chapter, the literature on IGE seems to be remarkably rare. One of the few attempts to discuss the subject (Rosenthal, 1984) comments on the managerial aspects of IGE but concludes that "the most realistic and valuable metaphor for evaluation of intergovernmental programs is that this activity itself become part of a broader societal learning system." We could therefore use two models (managerial and societal learning) to explain the utility of IGE and finally to assess the relevance of this sort of evaluation. In other words, these two models could be called social engineering and social enlightenment. However, we need to add a third model of utilization which applies to evaluation in general and which poses special problems in the case of IGE: this third mode can be termed democratic, (Duran and Monnier, 1992). In this third model, evaluation mainly aims at strengthening the accountability of governments. We will briefly deal with managerial, societal learning, and democratic models in turn.

The first model (managerial) applies to IGE only when the policy under evaluation is itself intergovernmental. The central evaluation question is worded as follows: to what extent is the intergovernmental policy or program a successful one? This model focuses on information feedback aimed at controlling implementation and marginally improving the design.

Managerial use of evaluation in intergovernmental environments faces serious problems since misunderstanding and misinterpreting the meaning of data will likely increase the further the analyst moves away from the source of information, and the more disparate the data sources become. Intergovernmental relations are paradoxical: they call for extensive information feed back but pragmatic constraints means that the data are of little value (Rosenthal, 1984).

The diversity of partners is likely to result in poor comparability. Time schedules and beneficiary areas may not be coherent, statistical definitions may have different meanings, and last but not least, different values may produce shifts in the goals assessed, the categories of impacts or the judgment criteria.

A further difficulty of using IGEs at the higher level becomes apparent when the time comes for synthesizing different local evaluations. In the case of European Structural Policies, the task is so difficult that the upper level has begun to launch more and more single-government evaluations and relies on them rather than on synthesizing conclusions drawn from IGEs. When confronting the problems of information feedback, we can ask whether intergovernmental evaluation is in fact an appropriate choice.

In the second model (societal learning), the intergovernmental evaluation becomes part of a broad societal learning system rather than a one-shot, clear-cut assessment of success or failure (Rosenthal, 1984). This model applies, to some extent, when a community with a common policy exists. The basic assumptions underlying the policy are presumably shared by the whole society, including politicians and officials at both levels of government. Evaluation is assumed to improve the understanding of the common political system and to transform that system in an incremental way. This function of evaluation is reflected in Karl Popper's perspective of incremental improvements in societal institutions and programs (Popper, 1963). It goes beyond organizational learning, and even beyond governmental learning, which Rist (1993) describes as a part of a web of interacting forces, power systems and institutional arrangements.

It could be claimed that such a societal use of evaluation is likely to develop in contexts where intensity of conflict is modest. This type of evaluation can only lead to utilization when it handles questions which are viewed as debatable by both levels of government.

This model could also be called one of "shared conceptual use." It seems to follow the rule of symmetry that applies to intergovernmental relations, but dissymmetries are observable in the framework. For example, during the Thatcher years, the British government used evaluation openly, especially performance indicators and "value for money audits," as a tool for diffusing neoliberal and managerial ways of thinking in the culture of local governments (Henkel, 1991)

In the democratic model, evaluation is a means to keep society and political personnel informed of policy effectiveness and relevance. In this case, both levels of the government concerned naturally attempt to justify their policies (if policies are competing) or the value they add to the common policy (if policies are intergovernmental). As a consequence, delicate questions can arise such as the extent to which each level contributes to the effectiveness of the policy as a whole or what is the relevance of the outcomes for the electorates at both levels?

In their efforts to provide proof of their respective utility, both levels of government may claim to have produced the same outcomes. If separate evaluations are carried out by each government, they will rapidly loose their credibility for trying to milk the same cow twice. Consequently, for the sake of credibility there has to be intergovernmental interaction in the evaluation process.

However, launching a common evaluation might raise other difficult problems since such an IGE can quickly show itself to be a zero-sum game. Competing levels are likely to resort to strategies that will, they hope, prove beneficial to themselves: retaining data, undermining the credibility of evaluators, gambling with successive goals, and censoring sensitive questions (Patton, 1986). If accountability is at stake, there must be some intergovernmental features in the evaluation. However, it is likely that interaction between levels will become weaker as the evaluation gets closer to the public arena, for high visibility creates more political vulnerability.

A Final Word

It is clear that among the different kinds of evaluation, IGE appears to be the most vulnerable to high political intrigue. Governments are defined by their autonomy in the use of political resources. Intergovernmental relations are defined by a symmetry in powers. IGE implies certain political agreement on agendas, terms of reference, evaluation methods, intended use of the findings, and so on. But this is not always so. And when this is the case, on what ground can IGE stand?

References

Duran, P. and E. Monnier (1992). "Le développement de l'évaluation en France, nécessités techniques et exigences politiques." *Revue française de sciences politiques*, 42/2.

Henkel, M. (1991). "The New 'Evaluative State.'" *Public Administration*, 69/1, 121–36.

Lobosco, A. and J. Kaufman (1989). "Working with State and Local Service Delivery Systems: The Politics of Evaluating Educational Opportunity Programs at the Community College Level." *Evaluation Review*, 13/2, 141–56.

Patton, M.Q. (1986). *Utilization-Focused Evaluation*. Newbury Park, CA: Sage.

Popper, K.R. (1963) Conjectures and refutations. London: Routledge and Kegan Paul; New York: Basic Books.

Rhodes, R.A.W. (1981). *Control and Power in Central-local Government Relations*. Aldershot: Gower Publishing Company. This book includes a comprehensive international bibliography covering the 1960s and the 1970s.

Rist, R.C. (1989). "Managing of Evaluations or Managing by Evaluations: Choices and Consequences." In R.C. Rist, ed., *Program Evaluation and the Management of Government : Patterns and Prospects across Eight Nations.* New Brunswick, NJ : Transaction Publishers.

Rist, R.C. (1993) "The Preconditions for Learning: Lessons from the Public Sector." In F.L. Leeuw, R.C. Rist, and R.C. Sonnichsen, eds., *Can Governments Learn? Comparative Perspective on Evaluation and Organizational Learning.* New Brunswick, NJ: Transaction Publishers.

Rosenthal, S.R. (1984). "New Directions for Evaluating Inter-governmental Programs." *Public Administration Review,* 44/6, 469–76.

Scharpf, F. (1988). "The Joint-Decision Trap: Lessons from German Federalism and European Integration." *Public Administration,* 66/Autumn, 239–78.

Sharkanski, I. (1981). "Intergovernmental Relations." In C. Nystrom and W. Starbuck, eds., *Handbook of Organizational Design.* Oxford: Oxford University Press.

Simeon, R. (1972). *Federal-Provincial Diplomacy: The Making of Recent Policy in Canada.* Toronto: University Press.

Sinacore, J.M. and R.S. Turpin (1991). "Multisite Evaluations: A Survey of Organizational and Methodological Issues." *New Directions for Program Evaluation,* no. 50.

Wright, D.S. (1978). *Understanding Inter-governmental Relations.* North Scituate, MA: Duxbury Press.

1

Evaluation and Autonomy in Sweden

Jan Eric Furubo

Introduction: The Swedish Context

In this chapter we shall turn our attention to a system of political relationships in Sweden, the country that for a number of years has had the largest public sector of all the OECD countries in terms of tax share. A large proportion of this politically regulated use of resources takes place within a framework where various national programs provide fundamental guidelines while policy implementation lies with Swedish local government bodies, in the shape of the municipal local authorities and the regional county councils.

A good proportion of evaluation activity at the national level may be regarded as dealing with this local and regional implementation and its effects in relation to various national goals. Local authorities participate in the evaluation process as providers of information, of course, but they also make use of the results. At the same time, the local authorities have their own evaluation activities partly based on criteria derived from national policy.

This is not a new situation. What is new, however, is the intended use of follow-ups and evaluations conducted at the national level. Previously they were intended for use as factual materials for policymaking at national level and for decisions at the same level concerning ways of changing local authority implementation. The choice of criteria and methods for evaluation activities was subordinated to this user perspective.

Now, however, their use is more strongly linked to local authorities. The intention is that in the first instance local authorities will be able to use the evaluations to fuel their decision-making processes. Evaluation has become an instrument for the realization of autonomy.

A number of conditions necessary to speak of an intergovernmental relationship were discussed in the introductory chapter. Before going into details, we shall briefly describe the interactions between central, regional, and local government in Sweden.

Sweden has a regional level of government (the county councils), whose principal responsibility is health care, and a local level. The local level, which will be the main focus of our attention here, comprises some 275 municipal local authorities. These authorities have the power to impose taxation on those residing within their jurisdiction. In fact, the overwhelming majority of Swedes only pay tax on income to their local authorities (and county councils). In many local authorities this amounts to some 30 percent of aggregate revenue.

Every local authority has its own representative assembly. These are chosen in elections with approximately the same voter turnout as parliamentary elections. Taken as a whole, all these factors mean that local authorities possess a significant degree of autonomy. They have the means to take on many tasks on their own initiative. In a number of areas they are obliged to discharge certain tasks in order to achieve national policy goals. But even in this connection they have considerable freedom to choose their means of implementation and their levels of ambition.

We may therefore regard Swedish local authorities as fairly autonomous bodies. This is also consistent with their historical development. They did not originate solely for the purpose of organizing the local administration of certain matters previously regarded as the concern of central government. This aspect is admittedly present in the historical picture, but it is by no means the only one. The local authorities evolved to provide a way to organize the common management of the common concerns of individuals in a town or a district. Thus there are elements of self-government, with towns and villages having early on acquired freedoms lacking in many other countries (Larsson, 1992, p. 46).

A concept such as autonomy is admittedly difficult to define with any precision. Above all, it is difficult to operationalize. We shall, however, attempt to pin down a number of characteristics in the relationship between central government and local authorities. In Sweden, there is considerable evidence of the trend mentioned in the Introduction towards growing autonomy in Nordic and other countries, at least on a rhetorical level. But certain concrete, significant changes in recent years have also been motivated using arguments relating to municipal autonomy.

Until recently, central government grants to local authorities, amounting to some 20 percent of aggregate municipal revenue, were used to support an extensive system of grants for different local authority activities. Along with the money, the local authorities received fairly detailed directives on how it should be used, with the aim of urging local authority activities to take a particular direction. The system has now been replaced by a more general system of central government grants taking account of the unevenness of the tax base in different local authorities. The system of grants is also no longer intended or expected to regulate the actions of local authorities.

The actual form taken by the relationship between central government and local authorities is different in different areas of policy. But in general terms it can be said that the relationship between them should be such that it creates an interest in results more than in processes. Therefore the development of the relation between the government and the communities has taken the same direction as the general development of the public sector in Sweden (Sandahl, 1993; Furubo 1994).

The character of the relationship in a given area of policy is, of course, dependent on the historical development of local authority activities. It is not irrelevant to ask whether activities in a particular area of policy evolved over a long period of time, only later taking the form of a more comprehensive national policy, or whether they originated with a national policy of which local authorities were regarded as implementers.

The first case involves the execution of policies that may be said to be self-imposed and whose norms and criteria are those of the local authority. In the other case the role of the local authority is more unambiguously that of an implementer, and the national level would in principle be able to choose other implementers. This second case equates fairly closely to what is defined in the Introduction as "interorganizational relations." In reality, however, it would seldom be possible to classify local authority activities in one or other of these clear-cut categories. We should rather regard them as extremes of a continuum. It is probably true that most public sector activities have arisen through a fairly complex interaction between national and local levels, with the role of initiator shifting back and forth between the two. In this connection, the national association of local authorities that has long existed in Sweden has played and continues to play a significant role.

We intend to make one single area of policy the main focus of the present chapter, which we shall conclude with some more general reflections. This particular area of policy has almost certainly been shaped to a high degree by an interaction between local and central initiatives of the type mentioned above. Alongside social welfare and, in a broad sense, health care, the system of primary and secondary education constitutes one of the most cost-intensive activities of the public sector. Since the 1970s, the share of the GNP consumed by primary and secondary education has amounted to between 4 percent and a little over 5 percent. Approximately 1.3 million students attend primary and secondary schools. In all, there are somewhat fewer than 500 compulsory schools and slightly more than 500 upper secondary schools. This means that every local authority, with the exception of the very smallest, administers a significant number of schools. Quite a few local authorities have dozens of schools within their jurisdiction. Within local authorities, the schools are administered by a politically representative committee appointed by the democratically elected municipal assembly.

The Intergovernmental Education System

The provision of education for the young—a compulsory nine-year school and a noncompulsory two- to four-year upper secondary school—has long been regarded in Sweden as a local authority concern conducted within the framework of a national policy. However, as regards the actual distribution of responsibility between central government and local authorities, a very marked change occurred in the early 1990s.

Prior to this, the local authorities may be considered executors of central government educational policy. A comprehensive system of central government grants for various purposes was intended to regulate the actions of local authorities in different ways. In all, there were thirty-five of these earmarked central government grants, and some 100 grant-related ordinances regulating the use to which the money could be put (Lundh, 1994, p. 4).

In 1991, these grants were replaced by a simplified, more generic system of grants. Then, in 1993, all correlation between, on the one hand, the activities of local authorities in relation to schools as well as factors influencing these and, on the other, the amount of money received by local authorities, was completely abolished. Central government support for schools was incorporated into a general tax equalization grant that supplemented the tax revenue of local authorities and was to be paid to them regardless of the activities they carried out. In essence, the equalization grant is intended to level out differences in tax base and in costs arising for reasons beyond the control of local authorities, such as the demographic structure, climate, and so on.

With this development, central government no longer has at its disposal financial instruments for shaping local authority activities in the school sector.

The autonomy of local authorities in the school sector has grown in other ways too. Before this new trend, whose arrival coincided with the onset of the 1990s, central government also specified the number of periods allocated to different subjects and laid down curriculum content and the educational methods for which detailed plans were provided. The purpose of the new curricula that have now been introduced into schools is not to focus "the utilization and designation of time", but rather "the results attained and the constant endeavor to improve educational methods". The curricula now in force make it clear what students are expected to know when they have completed a subject or a course of study that constitutes a part of their education. The curricula are there to identify the purpose, goals and structure of the subject or course. On the other hand, they are not supposed to contain instructions with respect to methods or the selection of material. Thus, the curricula "must to clear about the knowledge students should possess when they leave school, but they should leave ample room for teachers to select material and methods of instruction in accordance with the needs of the students and local preconditions" (Riksrevisionsverket, 1994).

The curricula are thus goal-related. The way and the extent to which different subjects are treated is left to the individual teacher. The syllabus may be said to address itself directly to professionals active in the school system. It does not address the local authorities at administrative or political level.

At the national level, there is also a system of examinations with a dual purpose. It provides diagnostic information while giving teachers an opportunity to calibrate their students' grades. However, at this national level, it does not provide information appropriate for the regulation of individual local authorities.

Grading students is compulsory from the seventh year (thirteen to fourteen year olds). Local authorities are able to decide for themselves, however, if they wish to introduce grading earlier than this.

As regards the competence of teaching staff, the criteria for professional teaching qualifications are laid down at the national level, but the local authorities themselves are free to decide the proportion of qualified and nonqualified staff.[1]

Local authorities have thus obtained extensive powers to organize their schools as they see fit. Local authorities may also profile different schools to emphasize different educational characteristics, thereby adding goals of their own with respect to all the schools in the municipality or to individual schools. This may actually entail widely differing implementations of the general national policy for schools by different local authorities.

The national level also lacks real sanctions. Parliament can theoretically decide to take over the administration of schools from any individual local authority, but as one official put it: "It's not atom bombs you need, but weapons of a finer calibre."

In sum, it may be said that the power to interpret a given regulation—in this case the right to interpret national goals—has to a great extent been shifted from the national level to the local authorities and indeed to school managers and teachers. The power of interpretation remains at the national level for certain unambiguous national obligations that local authorities are compelled to discharge, such as compulsory school attendance and observance of the fundamental goals of the general syllabuses.

Evaluations Underpin the System

Our example taken from the educational sphere constitutes a case of multilateral relations. In this system, local authority autonomy in the school sector is ultimately based on the confidence that the political processes are such that political representatives really place sufficient resources at the disposal of their schools in order to achieve the national goal of an educational system that is of equal value and attains equal standards throughout the country. In other words, the underlying assumption may be stated explicitly as follows: all those involved in the school system are enthusiastic partisans of its development and act rationally in the sense that they use the knowledge they acquire about various circumstances and correlations in their field to make the appropriate informed decisions.

This assumption in relation to motives and political and human behavior may be considered the basis of the importance attributed to follow-up and evaluation in the decentralized system sketched above. At the national level, therefore, the agency previously charged with the school system, which was oriented towards inspection, regulation surveillance, and so on, was transformed into a follow-up and evaluation body with the task of producing follow-up and evaluation information, which is then disseminated to those involved in the school system.

The former regulatory system also produced comprehensive materials based on follow-up and evaluation. It was of course important, at least in principle, for the national level to see how the various financial policy levers and the body of administrative regulations affected the operations of the school system. We may say, however, that this involved a purely top-down perspective. The information produced was to be used at the national level according to those criteria which had formed the starting point for the construction of the body of central government regulations.

As a matter of principle, the follow-up and evaluation information currently produced for the professionals in the school system and the political decision makers now has a different purpose. It is intended to provide those involved with briefing materials enabling them to make comparisons and giving them food for thought as a stimulus for personal reflections and judgments. Or, as one of the designers of the new follow-up and evaluation system puts it: "[I]n a deregulated and decentralized control system...the exchange of information between central government and the agencies responsible for the schools and the various local authorities is what fuels the development effort. It is assumed that comparisons will stimulate the discussion of organizational questions, the utilization of resources and the results obtained" (Lundh, 1994, p. 6).

Evaluations at Various Levels

National performance analysis in the form of follow-up and evaluation, with the fundamental perspective presented above, therefore has the goal of influencing decisions by local authorities. Not influencing the content as such in the decisions made by local authorities, but rather encouraging decisions to be made on the basis of more comprehensive factual evidence. At the same time, the information produced provides an indication of the situation at the national level. The questions being asked concern the quality of the school system as a whole, the development of the students' level of knowledge, and so on. In this way, the information should be useful in making general decisions about the school system, for example duration, design of syllabuses, and naturally, as an ultimate issue, the matter of local authority autonomy in the school sector.

National performance analysis is to be used at both national and local levels, including individual schools. In addition, follow-up and evaluation are carried out at the local level, and may involve performance analysis both within a local authority as a whole and within a single school. These local performance analyses are not carried up to national level. Instead, the idea is that follow-up and evaluation should be carried out in relation to the detailed, concrete goals obtaining for each individual local authority or school.

The Organization of National Evaluation Activities

The purpose of national evaluation activities is thus twofold: to provide information that may be relayed back to the local authorities at the same time as briefing materials to facilitate the taking of a policy position on the part of the national decision makers, and to ensure the provision of this information, a central agency has been set up with follow-up and evaluation activities as its principal purpose.

If we consider the intergovernmental profile of evaluation activities depicted in figures 1.1 and 1.2 in the introductory chapter, we may say that through this National Agency for Education, the national level dominates all the stages up to final use. Naturally, the task of collecting data often falls to the local level, but within the framework of the national body of regulations. Local authorities are obliged to provide statistical information to the National Agency. The information may concern the amount of money devoted to the school system, the competence of the teaching staff, the profiles adopted by different schools concerning, for example, the number of students per class, the number of students studying various languages, the number of students from immigrant families participating in the so-called home language tuition or similar activities, and the proportion of students participating in the different ability-streamed mathematics courses.

However, local authorities are under no clear-cut obligation to cooperate with more comprehensive evaluation programs which require access to individual schools to obtain information about individual students and groups of students, with a view to designing educational experiments, for example.

The control exercised by the national level over evaluation activities is thus considerable. It may be said that these evaluation activities are the most centralized aspect of a sector which in other respects has been completely handed over to local authority jurisdiction.

Kinds of Evaluation

What kinds of evaluation are produced by the National Agency for Education? The Agency has designed a special follow-up system within whose framework it continuously publishes data on the schools in the Swedish educational system. It issues special documents with comparative figures and descriptions of the situation in different local authorities. The documents may give data on variations in profile orientations in the schools, on the allocation of teaching resources with respect to different languages, the distribution of students studying different kinds of mathematics courses, student absenteeism, staff composition, etc. In this follow-up system, the performance, costs, and preconditions of the school system itself are thus the center of attention.

Other evaluation activities within the National Agency for Education are more oriented towards establishing causal relationships, such as the question of which factors of method and/or other educational input influence the skills and attitudes of the students. These activities may examine how well the teaching in the school system corresponds to certain national requirements, for example.

Experience Gained to Date

The intergovernmental system of evaluation described above has been in operation for a relatively brief period and, to some extent, is still in the process of development. But, apart from this reservation, how well has it worked? We are in a position to discuss the more continuous aspects of the evaluation system. In a report by the National Audit Office based principally on interviews and surveys conducted in local authorities, some problems have emerged. These will be briefly noted.

1. The Level of Reliability is Inadequate

The audit performed by the National Audit Bureau reveals that 41 percent of the local authorities experience problems with reporting data. In this connection, a number of local authorities point to difficulties relating to:

- the local authority's organization of school activities;
- the fact that the reporting must be adapted to the survey of the National Agency for Education;
- collection periods do not correspond to the periods when local authorities prepare their budgets and annual accounts; and
- there are time-consuming manual calculations.

Several of these comments by local authorities arise because they have integrated school activities with other municipal activities. This has mainly been the case between education and child care. In certain cases, school activities have been merged with recreational and cultural activities. These merged activities typically share rent, administration and management costs. The internal accounting systems are not designed to itemize the schools' share of the merged costs. This often entails calculating costs based on estimates reached by different methods.

Finally, there are indications that elected policymakers in the municipal executive committee fail to make clear demands on the local authority's system for reporting on educational activities. When policymakers are subsequently supplied with (or themselves obtain) comparative statistical data, extensive inquiries may be necessary to establish the degree of comparability with other local authorities of interest. The officials concerned must then interpret and analyze, on behalf of the policymakers, the information contained in the national follow-up. Otherwise, measures affecting education could be taken on partially erroneous grounds.

2. There are Validity Problems

Many local authorities consider the concepts and definitions employed in national follow-up work to be ambiguous. Approximately one fifth of the country's large and medium-sized local authorities experience difficulties of this kind. Six out of ten local authorities experience difficulties in certain cases, but state that the concepts and definitions used are 'for the most part' unambiguous. In their comments on this question, local authorities have given some thirty examples of concepts and definitions they judge to be ambiguous. Most of these concern:

- renting costs/square footage/utility area/internal rent;
- local versus central administration; and
- flexible starting age/pre-school preparatory activities.

3. It is Not Clear How the Follow-ups are Utilized

There are indications that data from the national follow-up have hitherto been utilized more as briefing material for discussions on savings in the field of education than as briefing material for reorienting priorities, boosting resources or other positive measures.

According to the review, 84 percent of local authorities have used results from the national follow-up in their activities. In most cases, the areas mentioned are: budget preparation and the allocation of resources, information for elected policymakers, discussions with head teachers and school staff, and comparison with other local authorities. One local authority said that it compared results with its own local follow-up results. Those local authorities who have still not used the national follow-up results argue, in the main, that these only became available a short time ago. The National Audit Office study shows that the national follow-up has not as yet been very effective in stimulating local authorities to make tangible changes in their educational activities. Only one or two local authorities have described concrete changes implemented as a result of information from the follow-up system.

Criteria and Conflicts

Information structures are discussed as a natural consequence of the fact that many different users must be able to "recognize themselves" in follow-ups and evaluations. And it is not implausible that the central and the local levels should have differing views as to what matters are of interest and by what value criteria they should be judged. Different users find different kinds of information useful, depending among other aspects on the openness of the decision-making situation. A reasonable hypothesis would therefore be that the selection of criteria in different evaluations and the orientation of evaluation activities will be affected by the level which controls the evaluations. It is conceivable, for instance, that the central level may have a greater interest in obtaining information which might lead to queries about local authority activities in the school sector.

However, a conflict of this nature does not appear to have surfaced in the discussion about the evaluation activities of central government and local authorities in the school sector. We interviewed representatives of the National Agency for Education and a number of local authorities while preparing this paper, and confirm that no conflict of this kind had emerged. On the contrary, it would seem that all those involved were interested in obtaining roughly the same kind of information.

Both local and central levels are interested in a continuous flow of information on the organizational, staff, and financial conditions under which the educational system works at the local authority level and also on the achievements of the local school system. As we have seen, 84 percent of local authorities state that they use data from national follow-up activities. Areas of use indicated in the majority of cases are budget preparation and the allocation of resources, information for elected policymakers, discussions with head teachers and school staff and comparison with other local authorities. But even at the local level there is interest in evaluations more oriented towards finding out the fundamental causal correlations which affect the educational system. This relative harmony may be connected with the fact that the school sector has powerful professional structures and pressure groups such as parents, teachers and others with a strong interest in developing the school system on the basis of current conditions rather than reassessing the whole system in a more fundamental fashion.

At the central level it is claimed that local authorities have shown a positive attitude towards the increased collection of information. One remark was: "The local authorities have reacted positively, they now consider all the data important because regulation takes place within the local authorities and they are concerned that their own local authority should be as good as possible." The only problem with the local authorities is that "they sometimes lack the expertise to carry out a deeper analysis of the data and they may not have reporting systems enabling them to gather the data they want." The National Agency for Education is, however, working on this problem by starting to 'train interested local authorities in the methodology of setting up such systems' (Riksrevisionsverket, 1993).

Bearing this in mind, evaluation activities participate to a great extent in different learning processes. This conclusion also harmonizes with the view that the information obtained from evaluation activities ought to stimulate "discussion of organizational questions, the utilization of resources and the results obtained"—see the earlier quotation from one of the designers of the current system of follow-up and evaluation.

Can this harmony be extended to infinity? We naturally have no final answer to this question. But we think we are in a position to make a number of reflections on the issue.

To a large extent, the collection of information we have described takes place within given limitations. The system presupposes that all concerned "want the school system to be as good as it possibly can." The evaluation activities at national level are also based on the need to know whether or not the goals set by central government are in fact being achieved. This places the information in a supervisory framework.

What, then, might happen if it were shown that the national goals were not being achieved? If, for instance, dramatic differences between local authorities were to arise, if certain local authorities neglected immigrant students, or if certain local authorities were to utilize teaching staff with dubious or no qualifications? So long as it remains a matter of individual local authorities, central government does have sanctions at its disposal, as we mentioned above, in the shape of the compulsory administration referred to by a national official as an "atom bomb."

But what if the problem were to become more general? What would happen then? Ultimately, this question takes us back to the problem of the nature of autonomy and the actual degree of irreversibility inherent in the processes of power distribution we have described.

If we assume that, as soon as things go wrong so to speak, central government will be able to recover the powers involved and say that after all it wasn't such a good idea to let the local authorities run the school system (for instance), then what we have described is conditional autonomy, a delegation which may be recalled at any moment. But the point at issue is whether central government will be able to recover the power it has now turned over to the local authorities. In our view, which is only that of individual citizens attempting to assess complex forces, central government will hardly be in a position to do so. In this sense the process in question involves real and newly won autonomy for local authorities.

Concluding Reflections

In this paper we have taken relationships within the school system as our starting point. The tendency towards a growing autonomy for local authorities and the significance of evaluation activities at the national level with regard to this autonomy, may be said to constitute a general, high-level trend in the development of Swedish administration.

In 1987, the Swedish Association of Local Authorities calculated that there were 108 different specifically allocated central government grants. In just a few steps these have been discontinued, being replaced as of 1 January 1993 by the government tax equalization grant to local authorities.

Within the various sectors of society, therefore, local authorities have been charged with providing data to the national level. Along with the school system, the social services sector in particular has come a long way in developing a national system of follow-up and evaluation. At regular intervals, the Government also intends reporting to Parliament on "activities financed by local authorities and county councils and provide as transparent an overview as possible." This report will also contain a "synthesis of how the general goals and the partial goals within each sphere of activity are being achieved."

In this connection, there is a difference between the changed information requirements resulting from delegation within central government and changed information needs resulting from the growing autonomy of local authorities. With respect to developments within central government, there has been an attempt to give central government agencies more and more autonomy in discharging their tasks. This attempt has been used as a reason for placing greater information demands on the agencies. The freedom is to be balanced by checks so that the Government will be able to take corrective measures if the agencies' activities do not develop in a desirable way.

Note that the matter involves delegating responsibilities to the agencies. Power still lies with the government and Parliament, and the delegation of some matters to the agencies may be regarded as more of a question of operational technique.

With regard to the relationship between central government and local authorities, the situation is different. Here, different political structures confront each other, each with its own popular mandate. It is not just a question of operational technique, but more a question of the level at which democratically based authority over various sectors of society, such as the school system, should be exercised.

The character of the information required by the central level varies depending on where we find ourselves on the scale from delegation to autonomy. The nearer we approach delegation, the more it is a question of information for the purposes of control. The nearer we approach autonomy, the less prominent this control purpose becomes. If there is no room for sanctions, as there will not be in the case of an autonomous relationship, there is little cause for control, either.

In Sweden, requirements for control information with respect to local authorities also seem to be subordinate to other kinds of information demands. The focus is rather on information on which to base the local authorities' own decisions, and as the representative of the National Agency for Education expressed it: "to provide food for thought."

Note

1. Not unexpectedly, this freedom has given rise to concern that local authorities would prefer to employ unqualified teaching staff for financial reasons, as they command lower salaries. A recently published report indicates that this has not occurred (National Agency for Education Report, no. 30).

References

Furubo, J.E. (1994). "Learning from Evaluations: The Swedish Experience." In F. Leeuw, R.C. Rist, R. Sonnichsen, eds., *Can Governments Learn? Comparative Perspectives on Evaluation & Organizational Learning*. New Brunswick, NJ: Transaction Publishers.

Larsson, T. (1992). Draft version of forthcoming book "Statssicket-Teori, Praktik och Problem."

Lundh, S. (1994). Memorandum about the evaluation-activities in the National Agency for Education.

Sandahl, R. (1993). "Connected or Separated. In A. Gray, W. Jenkins, and R. Segsworth, eds., *Budgeting, Auditing, Evaluating: Functions and Integration in Seven Governments*. New Brunswick: Transaction Publishers.

Riksrevisionsverket (1993). Memorandum about evaluations in the local authorities.

Riksrevisionsverket (1994). *Skolverket—central myndighet i ny roll.*

2

Evaluative Institutions in England and Wales: Weak Versions of Intergovernmental Evaluation

Mary Henkel

Introduction

Intergovernmental evaluation remains largely alien to British government. The problem lies both in the concept of evaluation and in the nature of government in this country. While forms of evaluative activity such as audit, inspection, performance measurement, cost effectiveness or "value for money" exercises, monitoring, and quality assessment have proliferated in the public sector during the 1980s and 1990s, there is no tradition of policy evaluation or policy analysis in British public administration. Unlike some other countries, there is, therefore, no consensus about what evaluation means and no established methodology. At the same time, the political thrust has been towards centralization or increasing asymmetry of powers between central and local government. Thus, although there are some public services, such as education and community care, which are subject to both local government and direct decentralized administration from central government, the criteria and mechanisms of evaluation have been set by central government and the role of local government has been subsidiary rather than interactive.

Policy Evaluation and British Government

There is a paradox in the British political system at the end of the twentieth century: that while evaluation is apparently an increasingly important instrument of public management, the radical changes to the policy framework within which evaluative activity has assumed such a high profile have been introduced primarily on the basis of political conviction rather than policy analysis.

The fate of attempts in the 1960s and early 1970s to install program and policy analysis in British government has been well documented (Gray and Jenkins, 1982; Garrett, 1972). The project of the Rothschild reforms (1971) to create a research commissioning system in central government that would harness research more effectively to the needs of the policy makers was not sustained, even where it was most strongly embraced, for example in the (then) Department of Health and Social Security (Kogan and Henkel, 1983). The idea that research might contribute to fundamental policy evaluation was never fully accepted. Moreover, although some efforts were made to include representatives of local government in structures for deciding priorities for research and evaluation, it was unquestionably a central government system, in which civil servants acted as proxy customers for local government.

Central government commissioning of research continues but, in the case of new policies, the emphasis is on how they are being implemented rather than on a critical examination of the policies themselves. A recent publication from a central government department (Department of Environment) which does move some way from this more narrow approach, still starts from the statement that "evaluation is a key management tool" (Doig and Littlewood, 1992).

In so far as policy evaluation is a feature of the British political culture, it is undertaken by researchers, either through independent funding or through sponsorship by central government; it is not an intergovernmental exercise. Key values underlying central government commissioning are efficiency and effectiveness within established objectives.

Intergovernmental evaluation in the sense of the involvement of central and local government is primarily program evaluation. It is most evident in the work of evaluative institutions established by government for the monitoring and evaluation of the performance of local government: inspectorates and the Audit Commission. They will constitute the main focus of this chapter. But first the context of intergovernmental relationships will be briefly described.

Central-Local Government Relations in Britain

During the 1960s and 1970s, central government became increasingly dependent upon local government and the relationships between the two were those of exchange and bargaining. However, since 1979 central government has sought to reverse the trend. It has not hesitated to assert its authority to redefine the nature and degree of intergovernmental dependencies and the institutions and structures within which they operate. It has drastically narrowed the discretion of local government in the use of power resources. The power of local government to raise revenue and to determine how it will spend its financial resources has been radically reduced and its financial dependence on central government commensurately extended. Only 20 percent of its resources now derive from local taxation. A tier of local government incorporating strategic functions and authority (metropolitan county councils) has been abolished. The hugely enlarged role of QUANGOs or Non-Departmental Public Bodies in British public administration is in part due to their assumption of functions removed from local government.

From 1979 to 1987, the new government's first objectives were the control of public expenditure, an assertion of strong government at the center and an erosion of local government power to pursue an alternative political agenda or undermine government priorities. A key component of this program for change was emphasis on the role of local government as manager of public resources and services and the embedding in it of a culture of management, centered on the values of economy, efficiency, effectiveness, and accountability to taxpayers.

Increasingly, during that period it seemed that the long-term objective might be the abolition of local *government* and the implementation of a "single government policy" through a combination of direct central administration, direct decentral administration and indirect administration (see Introduction) of national policies.

Since 1987 government has increasingly drawn up detailed, prescriptive national policies in areas previously left to local politicians, professionals, and bureaucrats (for example, education, training, and social care). But gradually the vision of local implementation structures has become less clear. The managerial solution has been absorbed into the more radical aims of privatization and the exposure of a shrinking public sector to market mechanisms and structures. But the concept (or more accurately, concepts) of the "enabling local authority" has emerged to compete with the idea that public policies can be implemented entirely through a collection of discrete QUANGOs, trusts, nonprofit organizations and private companies.

As originally proposed by Nicholas Ridley (1988) the "enabling authority" was defined in terms of local provision of services. Local authorities would cease to provide themselves and instead stimulate and regulate a market of suppliers through the issue of contracts on a competitive basis. Their role would thus be radically reduced to the development and awarding of contracts and to the assessment of contract compliance. The contract would thus become a key evaluative instrument through which efficiency and quality standards would be defined and enforced, albeit within a system framed by law and central government regulation.

However, the concept of the "enabling authority" has been redefined in a number of ways within both managerial and political perspectives (Cochrane, 1993) so that it is a contested idea. For Brooke (1989a and 1989b), local authorities will be strategic, developing a vision for their area and managing its realization through "a central core of strategic planners and regulators" and a whole range of independently managed single service agencies: a new version of the corporate planning and management ideas of the 1960s and 1970s. Others have seen it as a way of developing a local authority based on the notions of communitarianism and citizenship. They reject the idea of the authority enabling other organizations to do its work as too narrow. Rather they perceive the possibility of authorities "enabling communities to define and meet their needs" through being "close to the public as customer but also close to the public as citizen in determining public purpose" (Stewart, 1992, quoted in Cochrane, 1993). Others, again, focus on the need for local authorities to be more businesslike; to develop partnerships with business, defining, promoting and realizing the welfare of their residents on the basis of local economic prosperity (Cochrane, 1993).

The Role of Evaluation

Within this evolving, and to some extent still uncertain, agenda, what has been the role of evaluation and evaluative bodies? In particular, in so far as the idea of intergovernmental evaluation has any place in Britain, is it firmly embedded in a top-down managerial model?

During the 1980s the thesis that evaluative mechanisms were to be instruments of the centralization of authority and of the control and reduction of local government was difficult to refute (Henkel, 1991a and b). The measurement of performance against clear objectives was at the heart of the Financial Management Initiative for more accountable management in central government (Cmnd 8616, 1982). Performance indicators proliferated in every part of the public sector through the 1980s (Cave et al., 1988; Pollitt, 1986, 1990; Carter, 1991). The development by the Audit Commission of local authority profiles was a case in point. These provided a quantitative framework within which the detailed performance of local authorities could be compared, particularly on the criteria of economy and efficiency. The potential for central government to link that with resource allocation was evident.

However, in the 1990s evaluation took a rather different direction. There was a change of emphasis from economy to quality criteria in public services. With the introduction of quasi-markets in the public sector, policies of competition between public and private provision, and the idea of control by contract, there was a shift towards the encouragement of internal evaluative mechanisms. Local authorities, for the most part, did not cease to provide services. Instead they were divided into purchasers and providers and themselves entered the market place of provision. This has led to the installment of more local inspection units, internal performance review, quality assurance systems, quality improvement or total quality management as authorities seek to equip themselves to compete. The drive to develop measures of output and outcome has continued but stress has been laid on them as tools for self monitoring and self evaluation as well as for external appraisal and comparison.

Along with these developments came a broadening of the concept of accountability; a focus on standards, measures, and performance indicators as means by which the public could judge public services, make more informed choices about their use, and gain redress when they failed to deliver. These purposes were encapsulated in the Citizen's Charter (1991). Increasingly policies have been promulgated in the language of user involvement, user empowerment, user choice. Citizens as users or consumers of services will play a part in stimulating competition between service providers but to do that they will need information about their performance, league tables of school and university performance, and published reports on the quality of residential care, for example.

Against this background, the rest of the chapter will focus on two evaluative bodies representative of the two main types of public evaluative institution in Britain: inspectorates and audit. It will draw on examples primarily from one policy sector, that of the personal social services, and center on the period 1982–1994. It will compare and contrast the development of the two bodies and explore the ways in which their work can be accommodated within a framework of intergovernmental evaluation.

The Social Services Inspectorate and the Audit Commission have different origins, different authority and institutional status. Their creation and their methodologies reflect more determined attempts to reinforce central government authority and the more uniform implementation of national policies. At the same time, their modes and style of work have moved some way towards collaboration and incorporation of local authorities rather than imposition of a wholly summative and managerial model of evaluation.

The Social Services Inspectorate

Inspectorates were established in Britain in the nineteenth century as part of the growth of government. Two main forms have been identified by Rhodes (1981). Enforcement inspectorates, now to be found in central and local government, were introduced as a means of regulating private business in the name of public protection but as state involvement in all aspects of the economy grew, their remit was extended to the public sector.

The second, much smaller category of efficiency inspectorates, with which we are concerned, is part of the machinery of central government and concerned with the performance of public bodies at subcentral government level in the provision of services such as education, the public care of children and other vulnerable groups, the police, and fire services.

Originally centered on the inspection or direct scrutiny of, for example, poor law institutions and schools, the activities of these inspectorates gradually became more diffuse. By the 1970s they included as well fact finding, dissemination of good practice, mediation between central and local authorities, and the provision of policy advice to central government. They tended to be staffed by professionals from the relevant service and their models of evaluative practice were nearer those of peer review than of inspection. Their tasks were seen as collaborative development and gradual change within broadly agreed, if largely implicit, norms rather than the imposition of explicit central standards. They were part of an exchange relationship between central and local government in which it was assumed that policies and best practice in public services were predominantly developed at local level by an increasingly professionalized workforce who must be given discretion. In return, local government would provide services needed by the state.

In the 1980s many such assumptions began to change and as part of this change the regulatory and normative functions of Inspectorates were to be given a higher profile. They were to aid the government in its quest for increased economy, efficiency, and effectiveness in the public sector. They were expected to explicate clear criteria and standards of good practice and ensure adherence to these in more comprehensive programs of inspection than had been the norm.

At that time there was no inspectorate in the Department of Health and Social Security (DHSS) for the personal social services. However, in 1985 the Social Work Service, a professional advisory body, was converted into the Social Services Inspectorate (SSI) by decision of the secretary of state. Unlike some other efficiency inspectorates, it has no independent legal authority. It is a division of the (now) Department of Health. Inspectors are located in the London headquarters of the Department and six regions.

The remit of its predecessor advisory service (the Social Work Service) had included some statutory forms of inspection (of residential institutions). But much of its work was based on evaluation as a means of intergovernmental and interorganizational learning, realized through a collaborative approach with local authorities to the evaluation agenda. Negotiations were at regional level and often directed towards the needs of individual authorities. The evaluative mode was primarily formative. This was consistent with the dominant view that policymaking in the personal social services was primarily bottom-up and incrementalist.

While the new body would retain a role in policy advice, the main thrust of the mandate given to it in 1985 was "to assist local authorities to obtain value for money through the economic and efficient use of resources." Professional resources were included in this formula and the notion of interorganizational learning was retained in the injunction to identify good practice and spread knowledge about it. But promoting the improvement of the management of the personal social services was now a key responsibility of the Inspectorate and far more of its work would be structured through a national program of inspections that would be planned annually.

Since 1990, the SSI has been given increased responsibilities to monitor, and provide national guidance and assistance in, the implementation by local authorities of major new central government policies. In 1992, the SSI was restructured so as to make a clearer division between these responsibilities and its inspection work and to reinforce its decision to devote half of its resources to inspection. "SSI inspections systematically investigate the quality of services received by users and their carers and the management arrangements for the delivery of those services" (SSI, 1993). There are three main types of inspection:

- *Type 1*: those carried out, in some cases in an annual cycle, in the exercise of statutory duties and powers;
- *Type 2*: those undertaken without statutory mandate but at the request of, or in agreement with, an individual authority.
- *Type 3*: those undertaken without statutory mandate by agreement with the local authorities concerned and incorporated in a national program covering each year between twenty and thirty different forms of social care provision (for example, day services for people with mental illness, family centers for children and parents) or issues (for example, the needs of those caring for dependent relatives at home, equal access to services for ethnic minorities). Inspections would normally be conducted in a sample of local authorities (Henkel, 1991a).

In addition, regional inspectors might continue to establish programs of work with the social services departments, and increasingly, agencies in the independent sector, in their areas, either to follow up national inspections or in pursuit of more local priorities.

The national inspection program has several aims: to examine the quality of service provision across the country against common criteria, to identify and disseminate good practice and to point up common problems. Evaluative criteria are determined by "government policy, regulation and legislation," ideas of "best practice" and research (SSI, 1993). These criteria, together with any indicators, measurements or conceptual frameworks and standards developed in the course of inspection, are then available for use by the local authorities themselves in internal inspections and as part of quality assurance. Sometimes the development of such criteria and measures are the primary focus of inspections (SSI,

1989). The institution of this national program thus represents a shift towards standardization and summative modes of evaluation. It will be examined more closely and compared with national studies undertaken by the Audit Commission.

The Audit Commission

The creation of the Audit Commission under the Local Government Finance Act (1982), was the means by which the British government modernized audit in England and Wales, first in local government and then (1990) in the National Health Service. The Commission, an independent body, is appointed by the secretaries of state for the environment, for health and for Wales and comprises up to twenty members "drawn from—but not representing"—industry, local government, the health and accountancy professions and the trade unions (Audit Commission, 1993). It has a management board consisting of the Controller and six directors. Strictly, therefore, it carries out a key function on behalf of central government; it is not part of it.

Its mandate extends well beyond that of regularity audit to include ensuring that authorities make "proper arrangements for securing economy, efficiency and effectiveness" in the management of their resources. It sees itself as carrying out its work in three main ways: by appointing auditors to all health bodies and local authorities; by undertaking national studies which make recommendations for improving economy, efficiency, and effectiveness of services which can then be applied at local level; and by encouraging authorities to learn from each other (Audit Commission, 1993).

The creation of the Commission was widely perceived as a means of reining in local government and it has certainly worked to implement more effective external scrutiny of local authority performance against nationally agreed priorities. However, partly because of this perception of its purpose, the Commission from the beginning emphasized its independent status, used the authority it had been given under the Act which created it (section 27) to criticize central as well as local government and stressed its role in helping local authorities to adapt to change and to equip themselves for survival. It pointed to internal performance review as a key to achieving these aims. The tools and measures developed by the Commission, such as local authority profiles, could be used not only for external comparisons of performance but also internally to raise questions about how, why and with what results authorities were spending their money and to promote self evaluation.

The Commission has also always emphasized its role in enhancing the accountability of local authorities, but primarily to citizens as taxpayers and through its reports to local authorities themselves. More recently, it has been assigned a role in the promotion of the Citizen's Charter. The Commission now specifies indicators of performance (Audit Commission, 1993) which local authorities are obliged to publish (Local Government Act, 1992) to enable the public to make judgments about how well they are doing.

But the main focus here will be on its national program of special studies. These are of particular interest for a study of intergovernmental evaluation, not least because they may be studies of either local government activities or the impacts of central government policies on the performance of local authorities.

The national program of special studies is the responsibility of two directorates in the Commission: Local Government Studies and Health and Personal Social Services Studies.[1] The focus is on the relationship between systems and practice of management, the use of resources and policy and service outputs. Their reports form the basis of audit guides which are used by local auditors in their annual audit work with each authority.

The methodological framework for the studies has remained broadly the same since 1984. An aspect of a local authority or health service activity is identified with potential for substantial increase in the economy, efficiency, or effectiveness with which it is managed. It may be a relatively neglected area or it may be high profile, for example because it is the subject of major policy change. A study team is appointed, first to develop a specification for comparative study and then to test it in a sample of authorities. On these bases a national report is published, identifying common problems, proposals for change and reporting existing good practice. From this a more detailed, technical guide is constructed. Methods of work rely on a combination of quantitative expertise, research knowledge and methodological expertise and experiential knowledge.

Recently, the Commission has identified itself explicitly with an ex ante role in policy implementation as well as post hoc evaluation of performance or policy analysis. "It is one of the principal roles of the Commission, as external auditors, to make sure arrangements are in place when new legislation is brought into being to ensure that authorities are able to deliver value for money" (chairman's evidence to the Select Committee on Health, 1993, para 148). "Over the next 12 months the Commission's auditors will be working with social services inspectors.... to monitor and advise on ways of overcoming.... difficulties to implement this important legislation [community care]" (Audit Commission, 1992b). Thus, whereas a national study of the Commission, undertaken within its remit to examine central government policies and their implications for local government performance, made a key contribution to policy change in the field of Community Care (Audit Commission, 1986), its recent reports in this field (Audit Commission, 1992a; 1992b) have concentrated uncritically on the potential of new policy for service improvement. Its aim is to ensure that local authorities make it work.

In this field and elsewhere (Audit Commission and Her Majesty's Inspectorate of Schools, 1992a and 1992b) joint work between the Commission and inspectorates is one demonstration of the convergènce between inspectorates in government and the independent Audit Commission after an initial period of competition between them (Henkel, 1991a). Future plans include joint studies of whole services by the Commission and SSI.

Comparing National Inspections and National Audit Studies: An Intergovernmental Process?

The Evaluation Agenda

The Social Services Inspectorate is unequivocally part of government. It has no independent legal status, it is dependent for its survival on the government of the day and at its inception it was a vulnerable institution. Its staff had previously constituted an advisory body to government representing a weak profession. It increased its authority in both central and local government by its preparedness to adopt a less hands-off approach to the problems of local government and by moving towards government priorities and values. But its statutory powers of inspection are, nevertheless, limited. To mount its national program of inspection it must consult formally. Inspections are planned in a Joint Steering Group chaired by a senior civil servant and with representatives from the local authority politicians and social services managers. In a new initiative in 1993, three lay and consumer representatives were appointed to join the Steering Group (SSI, 1993).

The Audit Commission is appointed by central government but is formally independent of both central and local government. Its studies have legal authority and Commission members, in consultation with the controller and the relevant special studies directorates, decide on its agenda. However, it includes people with past and present connections with local government among its members. Moreover, a key strategy adopted by the Commission from early in its history was to establish strong networking with the local government and other policy communities in whose field it was operating. An important part of its success has been its choice of study topics salient to the needs of local authorities, achieved no doubt, in part, through the effectiveness of those networks.

The Evaluators

The Social Services Inspectorate has a relatively small staff, approximately 100 professional inspectors. They are drawn primarily from professional social workers who have become managers in the personal social services, although more recent policy has been to supplement their expertise by recruiting a small cohort of social researchers. The SSI also has a small budget and a relatively limited policy of secondments to the inspectorate and inspection teams. These are from voluntary and private social services agencies as well as from local authorities. The planning of the structure and methodology of inspections is, therefore, primarily in the hands of the SSI staff themselves, as are the inspections themselves, although, again, the SSI has just introduced a policy of including service users or ex-users in inspection teams. Local government is thus perhaps more weakly represented than in the past.

There have been notable exceptions to SSI dominance of inspections or projects but these have tended to be regional initiatives outside the national programs. A collaborative project between a regional team and six local authority departments produced one of the most widely used evaluative frameworks for local inspections and evaluations of residential care (SSI, 1989). Another region has taken the lead in establishing a more permanent collaborative working group including voluntary organizations and health authorities as well as local authority social services departments for the purpose of planning local inspection and development work (SSI, 1992).

The Audit Commission, by contrast, has always relied substantially on secondments in its special studies programs. Special studies teams comprise a small core group from the Commission together with a local auditor. Teams might then have one or two part-time advisers, an academic and/or someone with substantial experience of the field. Teams might also have as consultants top managers or other senior people nominated from the field, predominantly local government, who might typically give perhaps eight to ten days of their time to the study. The planning and framing of studies therefore constitute a strongly collaborative exercise with significant representation from local government.

Reports

The process through which the Audit Commission produces its reports involves substantial consultation through a three monthly review panel which includes a small number of Commission members and senior representatives from the field. Draft reports are circulated to key groups in the policy network, including the local authority associations.

The SSI reports are the subject of less wide consultation, although participating local authorities receive the draft and are invited to comment on its factual accuracy.

In both cases, national reports are aimed at a wide audience in the policy network, although the Commission perceives its potential audience in broader terms than does the Inspectorate and includes local electorates. SSI's work is aimed primarily at managers and practitioners of services, although it is now aimed at being useful to service users (SSI, 1993).

Both the Commission and the SSI have invested in dissemination. In the case of the Commission this was built into the methodology of special studies from the beginning in a highly structured way. National reports would be converted into audit guides for use by local auditors in their annual audits in the local authorities. The aim was to identify means of economizing and improving the management and use of resources and to set goals for their achievement, which would be subject to further review. However, they have recognized that such a top-down rationalist structure is inadequate on its own to achieve major change.

The SSI's approach has evolved over time and is much more diverse. Sometimes inspections are part of a longer-term, more broadly conceived plan for investigation and preliminary analysis, inspection and then development work, in which both arms of the inspectorate might be involved over a period of years. In other cases, there might be follow-up work by regional inspectors with their authorities. Alternatively national conferences might be mounted to consider the implications of inspection reports.

Conclusions

This chapter has reviewed the work of two evaluative institutions in a context in which local government has become increasingly dependent on central government. Their work can be said to have contributed towards installing a model of government in which policies are set by, and belong to, national government; the function of local government is to implement them, and also to accept a significantly reduced role in the policy system. Local authorities are being pressed to surrender their role in providing services. But at the same time, the form of representative democracy which they embody is being supplanted by government, as it seeks to establish a new pluralism at local level. Thus the Social Services Inspectorate is incorporating independent agencies and service users into consultative procedures which were previously largely bilateral, between central and local government. The Audit Commission is a governing body drawn from multiple interests. It is also playing a part in diversifying forms of accountability.

But at the same time, several models of the local authority remain in the policy arena (Cochrane, 1993; Cordingley and Kogan, 1992). The potential of other players, at least at the service interface, to exert any significant degree of influence is untested. Diversity of values, policies, and structures remains a strong feature of local government and innovations still derive largely from the field. And while the evaluative institutions described have certainly contributed to a centralization of values and policies, they also recognize the complexities of policy implementation. Networking and consultation are increasingly evident in their evaluative processes. What could be said to be developing is a managerial model of intergovernmental evaluation but one which incorporates different conceptions of management (rationalist; negotiative; top-down; interactive; interorganizational learning).

These two evaluative institutions are examples of a weak version of intergovernmental evaluation. Local government provides the bulk of the Audit Commission funding from its audit fees but the framework of rules for both audit and inspection is laid down at the center. Central evaluative bodies consult with representatives from subcentral government on the agenda of inquiry and the key evaluative questions. They also incorporate local managers or professionals in their teams but they are not required to do so. The Audit Commission has established a strongly structured methodology in which members of special studies teams or local auditors carry the responsibility for data collection, data processing, and the production of the report. The Social Services Inspectorate has a more flexible approach to methodology but again retains control of the production of the report. Local bodies are deemed to be the prime users of the evaluation and it is at the point of utilization that most interaction between them and the evaluative institutions is expected. But even here, a new set of players has now been introduced, citizen users. In theory, they might exploit the forces of the market to influence implementation or be used by the center to put pressure on local bodies to act on report findings, thus weakening collaborative interaction between the central and local government at this point.

There is no doubt that essentially the audit and inspection programs belong to the center. This would also be true of other forms of public evaluation in Britain.

Note

1. It is of interest that the division of responsibility between these directorates cuts across the administrative location of the audited organizations, in the name of functional coherence. While the National Health Service is managed by a chief executive directly accountable to the secretary of state for health and social services, the personal social services are the responsibility of local government.

References

Audit Commission (1986). "Making a Reality of Community Care." London: HMSO.

Audit Commission (1992a). "Community Care: Managing the Cascade of Change." London: HMSO.

Audit Commission (1992b). "The Community Revolution: Personal Social Services and Community Care." London: HMSO.

Audit Commission (1992c). "Getting in on the Act: Provision for Pupils with Special Needs: the National Picture." London: HMSO

Audit Commission (1992d). "Getting the Act Together: Provision for Pupils with Special Needs." London: HMSO

Audit Commission (1993). "Report and Accounts." London: HMSO.

Brooke, R. (1989a). *The Enabling Authority—Practical Consequences*, Local Government Studies, 15 (5).

Brooke, R. (1989b). *Managing the Enabling Authority*. London: Longman.

Carter, N. (1991). "Learning to Measure Performance: The Use of Indicators in Organizations." *Public Administration*, vol. 69, no.1 (Spring).

Cave, M., S. Hanney, M. Kogan, and G. Trevett (1988). *The Use of Performance Indicators in Higher Education: A Critical Analysis of Developing Practice.* London: Jessica Kingsley Publishers.

Cm 1599 (1991). *The Citizen's Charter.* London: HMSO.

Cmnd 4814 (1971). *The Organization and Management of Government R & D.* London: HMSO (Rothschild Report).

Cmnd 5406 (1972). *A Framework for Government Research and Development.* London: HMSO.

Cmnd 8616 (1982). *Efficiency and Effectiveness in the Civil Service.* London: HMSO.

Cochrane, A. (1993). *Whatever Happened to Local Government?* Buckingham: Open University Press.

Cordingley, P. and M. Kogan (1992). *In Support of Education.* London: Jessica Kingsley Publishers.

Doig, B. and J. Littlewood (eds.) (1992). "Policy Evaluation: The Role of Social Research." London: HMSO.

Garrett, J. (1972). *The Management of Government.* Pelican.

Gray, A. and W. Jenkins (1982). "Policy Analysis in British Central Government: The Experience of PAR. " *Public Administration*, vol. 60, no.4 (Winter).

Henkel, M. (1991a). *Government, Evaluation and Change.* London: Jessica Kingsley.

Henkel, M. (1991b) "The New 'Evaluative State.'" *Public Administration*, vol.69, no.1 (Spring).

Kogan, M. and M. Henkel (1983). *Government and Research: The Rothschild Experiment in a Government Department.* London: Heinemann Educational Books.

Pollitt, C. (1986). "Beyond the Managerial Model: The Case for Broadening Performance Assessment in Government and the Public Service." *Financial Accountability and Management*, 2(3).

Pollitt, C. (1990). "Performance Indicators, Root and Branch." In M. Cave, M. Kogan, and R. Smith, eds. *Output and Performance Measurement in Government: the State of the Art.* London: Jessica Kingsley.

Rhodes, G. (1981). *Inspectorates in British Government.* London: Allen and Unwin.

Ridley, N. (1988). *The Local Right: Enabling not Providing.* London: Center for Policy Studies.

Social Services Inspectorate (1989). *Homes are for Living In: A Model for Evaluating Quality of Care Provided and Quality of Life Experienced in Residential Care for Elderly Persons.* London: HMSO.

Social Services Inspectorate (1992). *Concern for Quality: the First Annual Report of the Chief Inspector, Social Services Inspectorate 1991/1992.* London: HMSO.

Social Services Inspectorate (1993). *Raising the Standard: The Second Annual Report of the Chief Inspector, Social Services Inspectorate 1992/1993.* London: HMSO.

Stewart, J. (1992) "Guidelines for Public Service Management: Lessons not to be Learnt from the Private Sector." In Carter et al. eds. *Changing Social Work and Social Welfare*, Buckingham: Open University Press.

3

Evaluation in the United States: Cooperative But Not Intergovernmental

Linda G. Morra

Introduction

Elementary and secondary school education, unemployment insurance, job training for dislocated workers, drug abuse prevention and treatment, antismoking campaigns, AIDS-awareness, pesticide use, drug safety, air safety, meat inspection—it is difficult to find an area of life in which governments have not developed policies, and programs implementing the policies, to meet societal objectives. Apart from a few programs, such as the administration of the social security system, however, the federal government in the United States is not a direct provider of domestic public services. Nearly all public services are jointly financed and delivered through the fifty states, 39,000 general purpose, and 44,000 special purpose local governments (U.S. General Accounting Office, 1990).

Typically in the United States the several levels of government—federal, state, and local—form a complex partnership in developing, implementing, and funding policies and programs. New policies and programs often begin with legislation that is enacted by the federal government.[1] Once legislation is enacted, the relevant federal executive agency distributes federal funds for the program generally to the states but, in some cases, directly to local governments. Once a state receives the funds, it may retain funds to implement and/or administer the program or it may divide the funds among local governments that oversee activities in the states' various counties, cities, and towns. Usually legislation specifies how much and for what purposes funds can be retained by the state. From the initial consideration of a new program or the reconsideration of an existing program by the federal government, there is much interaction between the federal, state, and local levels. For example, as the Congress debates the merits of one program approach as opposed to another, federal legislators may consult with state officials to get their reactions to the idea.

This federal, state, and local partnership extends to the financing of policies and programs. However, the federal role in financing programs and services provided by state and local governments is relatively small overall. In 1987, for example, the states and localities spent $926.7 billion. In contrast, in fiscal year 1988, federal financial assistance to states and localities including grants, tax subsidies, loans, and loan guarantees, totaled about $165.3 billion. While exceptions exist such as Medicare, a federal health care program for the elderly, many government programs reflect a financing picture mirroring this disparity. In the United States, elementary and secondary public education, for example, has historically been largely under state and local control and funding with the federal government contributing about 5 to 7 percent of the dollars expended.

While the federal financing role has oftentimes been small, it has nonetheless been important. It has often served as new money to foster innovations through demonstrations, to provide new services or programs, or to increase services to specific groups, such as the economically disadvantaged.[2] With the federal dollars have come program and administrative requirements, called regulations, as conditions for receiving the federal funds.

In general, the federal government relies on the cooperation and goodwill of the state and local governments. Sometimes, however, the federal government preempts state and local laws. The three levels of government tend to operate in a hierarchical fashion with the policies of the "higher" level of government superseding the "lower." Yet, at the same time, rarely is action unilateral at either federal, state, or local government levels. The system is best viewed as a loose intergovernmental partnership in which responsibility is shared. However, when it comes to evaluating government policies and programs, the model has not held—even when the program itself is jointly funded.

Program evaluation involves the collection of information on the implementation, outcomes, and effectiveness of a program. It answers questions such as: To what extent is a program targeting its intended population? What services is it providing to whom? With what results? Do people who go through the program fare better than they would have without participating in the program? Evaluative information is critical for knowing whether or how a program should be modified, expanded, or abolished.

In the United States, the federal and state governments often fund the subordinate level of government (i.e., state or local, respectively) to provide services directly to the public or to develop and implement legislated programs. Most frequently, funding is joint. The federal funding, for example, may be contingent on the state funding a certain share of the program.

Informally, each level of government is accountable to its electorate for determining if the program it is funding is successful in achieving the objectives set for it. Thus, intergovernmental evaluation, where two or more levels of government fund, plan, conduct, and report the evaluation, might be expected to be the norm. However, this is not the case. In general, evaluations for federal purposes have been conducted and evaluations for state or local program oversight or management have been conducted too. But these have been separate studies.

Current Organization of Evaluation at the Federal Level

The principal units in federal level evaluation activities are the U.S. Congress, the Office of Management and Budget (OMB), the U.S. General Accounting Office (GAO), the various evaluation units within the executive branch agencies, and the contractors who perform evaluations for the executive branch of government.

The U.S. Congress,[3] a legislative body, and OMB, an executive branch agency, function as oversight agencies for implementation of federal policies and programs. Congress, as the legislative body, often requires the evaluation of particular programs in authorizing legislation.[4] It may specify that a particular agency conduct the evaluation and earmark funds or expect the agency to conduct the evaluation out of other appropriated funds. Frequently, the Congress requests that the GAO, its legislative "watchdog" agency, conduct a study. OMB has been described by Wye as the primary planning, policymaking, budget, and analytical support for the president as he manages the executive branch of the government

(Wye, 1992). OMB also provides guidance on how executive branch agencies are to carry out the evaluation function.

Executive branch agencies generally have one or more units that conduct program evaluations. Small agencies and large agencies with a relatively narrow scope of activity tend to have centralized evaluation units; large agencies and agencies with a wide range of activities tend to have decentralized evaluation units, each associated with a cluster of programs, and a centralized coordinating unit (Wargo, 1983). Wargo describes the primary evaluation functions of an agency as planning, coordinating, executing, and monitoring evaluations and disseminating their findings. A GAO survey that reported on the number of units in non-defense agencies indicating that they were engaged in program evaluation found 133 such units in 1984 (U.S. General Accounting Office, 1987).

Often, executive branch agencies employ outside firms, called contractors, to help execute the agency's evaluation functions. Profit and nonprofit research and evaluation organizations are the typical contractors.

Growth in Program Evaluation at the Federal Level

The history of program evaluation in the United States is not intergovernmental. And until the 1980s, it is largely a federal history. The rise of evaluation in the federal government cannot be attributed to a single event. While lists may differ in number and magnitude of influence, two events are generally included: outcome-driven budgeting systems and large government expenditures on programs designed to meet social needs.

The evaluation movement is frequently tied to the Planning-Programming-Budgeting-System (PPBS) (Nathan, 1988). During the 1960s, under President Johnson, PPBS had the objective of systematically evaluating and comparing the use of all government resources—all resources, that is, expended by one level of government (Nathan, 1988). All federal programs were to be arrayed with program outcomes specified so that one could see what one was buying with what federal dollars and make resource decisions accordingly (Hyde and Shafritz, 1979). OMB, which among other activities provides guidance on how executive offices are to carry out the evaluation function, coordinated this effort.

PPBS is especially significant in that it set out an accountability model. The goal was to make resource allocation decisions based on evaluative information. Thus, the federal government assumed a "command and control" role with respect to the states and localities it at least partially funded to develop and implement programs. It was not following a societal learning model that said to those whom it provided with funds: "Let's work together to determine what we have learned about government intervention in this area so that we can improve our efforts." Rather, it set up a potentially adversarial relationship between levels of government rather than a cooperative relationship necessary for intergovernmental evaluation.

The evaluation movement is also frequently tied to the much earlier period immediately following World War II that saw the beginning of large-scale programs designed to meet social needs (Rossi and Freeman, 1982). Expenditures for these programs were huge and consequently were accompanied by demands for knowledge of results. By the mid-sixties, some major federal legislation was requiring project evaluation. Often cited, for example, is the Elementary and Secondary Education Act of 1965 that required such an evaluation of projects funded under it (Provis, 1971).

Evaluation activity boomed during the 1970s. Again, there are multiple reasons. First, many of the evaluations mandated in the middle or late sixties actually were conducted in the seventies. Planning, developing, conducting, and reporting on the large-scale evaluations took time. For example, one of the first major U.S. demonstration and evaluation studies, the negative income tax experiments, were begun in the late 1960s, but the results were not seen until the 1970s (Nathan, 1988). As Nathan states, "The seeds of the evaluation movement were planted in the 1960s but were cultivated and bore their fruit a decade later" (Nathan, 1988).

A second reason for the evaluation boom was the Great Society programs initiated by President Johnson in the mid-1960s. Evaluations of these programs were wanted even if they did not have an evaluation component. Levine credits Senator Daniel Patrick Moynihan for much of the boom:

> The evaluation boom began in the 1970s under the Nixon administration, in large measure as a result of prodding from the now senior senator from New York, Daniel Patrick Moynihan, who as a Nixon staffer wanted to pinpoint what worked—and, even more, what did not work—in the programs of President Johnson's Great Society. (Levine, 1983)

Third, as indicated by Rist, Congress did not like having to rely solely on the executive branch findings and reports for its oversight, authorization, and appropriation responsibilities (Rist, 1990). It turned to one of its legislative agencies, the United States General Accounting Office (GAO), to do independent assessments of the effects of these large investments in social programs. Created by the Budget and Accounting Act of 1921 as an organization independent of the executive branch, GAO gained responsibility for auditing executive branch financial actions. As chronicled by Trask, into the 1940s GAO was known primarily as a voucher-checking agency, but with its original broad legislative authority and subsequent legislative changes, GAO's audit role expanded over time (Trask, 1991). The Budget and Accounting Procedures Act of 1950 changed GAO's role in mandating that accounting systems and financial reporting were responsibilities of the executive branch and that GAO should prescribe accounting standards and principals and help develop, review, and approve agency systems. By the 1950s GAO still dealt with financial issues, but increasingly conducted investigations, surveys, and inspections. Gradually, over the 1960s, more attention went to examining program objectives and accomplishments.

GAO's role in evaluation fully emerged over the decade of the 1970s. It started with 1967 legislation that mandated GAO to evaluate poverty programs carried out by the executive and by local public and private agencies to determine the extent to which these programs had achieved their objectives. GAO studied the Job Corps, Head Start, Community Action, and other programs. The poverty programs work demonstrated GAO's qualifications to do program evaluation and Congress endorsed and expanded GAO's program evaluation role in 1970 and 1974 (Trask, 1991). Major GAO evaluation activity included reviewing the effectiveness of the municipal waste water treatment construction grant program and the New Jersey negative income tax experiment. By the mid-1970s, GAO's growing expertise in this type of work resulted in its addressing diverse issues such as income tax withholding for military personnel and the cost-effectiveness of automobile safety devices (Havens, 1990). GAO had become a major player for the Congress in the field of program evaluation.

The 1980s Bring Decline in Federal Evaluation Activity

The evaluation world changed in 1980 when the boom abruptly ended. Some researchers indicate a general dissatisfaction with the evaluations brought by the 1970s. They took a long time and were expensive; some were found to have flawed methodologies; all could be critiqued; and, often, they raised more questions than they answered about the programs (Richardson, 1992). Havens (1992) views the problem of the fragility of program evaluation partly as a young function, far less firmly established than the accounting function which has had decades to develop rules, procedures, systems, and acceptance in public and private management sectors (Havens, 1992).

While some frustration may have existed with effectiveness evaluations, the factor typically cited for the decrease in evaluation is the Reagan Administration which began in 1980. For example, as strongly stated by Levine:

> The Reagan administration came into office with no felt need for information about its predecessors' programs. Combining strong ideology with the impressive intellectual efforts of a few conservative foundations, it based its programs on a different sort of evaluation, which asked not, How well does it work? but If it works, will it move America in the direction in which we were elected to move it. This absence of felt need for evaluation information, combined with strong budget reductions imposed by the administration on all government activities, has meant a sharp downturn—which sometimes resembles a death knell—for the evaluation industry. (Levine, 1983 in St. Pierre)

The Reagan administration did attempt to reduce the federal role in the intergovernmental system. Cuts in federal aid and reduced tax revenues limited the federal government's ability to undertake new social initiatives and to maintain existing ones. In addition, the administration initiated block grants to the states which as created in the Omnibus Budget Reconciliation Act of 1981 eliminated fifty-nine grant programs and consolidated almost eighty narrowly focused categorical grant programs into nine broad-based block grants. The administration also made systematic efforts to reduce the number of federal regulations and "unburden" state and local governments. Program evaluation suffered a corresponding decline.

OMB reflected the administration's attitude to evaluation. In 1983, for example, OMB, "the primary planning, policy-making, budget, and analytical support for the President as he manages the executive branch of government" (Wye, 1992), rescinded OMB Circular A-117, guidance on evaluation activities. Circular A-117 emphasized the importance of the role of evaluation in the federal government and specifically, in its overall management improvement and budget process. Wye indicates that a view emerged in OMB that evaluation "is overly academic, expensive, unfocused, and largely irrelevant to practical management concerns; and that it is in fact part of the superstructure supporting entrenched, ineffective, inefficient, costly social programs (Wye, 1992)." Throughout most of the 1980s, OMB's evaluation activity was minimal.

The GAO has documented what happened overall to federal program evaluation during the 1980s (U.S. General Accounting Office, 1989). In 1980, 180 units in non-defense agencies reported that they conducted program evaluation activities. By 1984, this figure had decreased to 133. Professional staff in executive agency evaluation units decreased overall by 22 percent, from about 1,500 to about 1,200, between 1980 and 1984, while total staff for the agencies as a whole decreased only 6 percent. A 1988 study of fifteen units that were active in 1980 showed a 52 percent decrease in professional staff, an additional decrease of 12 percent since 1984.

Likewise, GAO showed the decrease in program evaluation funds. Funds for program evaluation decreased by 37 percent between 1980 and 1984 (in constant 1980 dollars), while agency budgets actually had an overall increase of 4 percent. The GAO also found that the same types of studies were not being done in 1984 and 1988 as had been done in 1980. Work shifted, the GAO reported, from complex evaluations that give more precise measures of program effects to less complex studies and nontechnical reports.

The GAO reported again in 1992 on the state of program evaluation (U.S. General Accounting Office, 1992). While the GAO did not repeat its survey, it indicated that its discussions with departmental officials offered no evidence that the executive branch investment in program evaluation showed any meaningful overall increase from 1988 to 1992. GAO concluded that the limited capacity for program evaluation in the executive branch has some important consequences in terms of agencies (1) lacking information on the effectiveness of programs they manage; (2) lacking data on the targeting and outreach of their programs; and (3) needing to improve their capacity to make sound decisions on the use of data for policymaking.

While in 1994 OMB is again supporting the concept of evaluation, staff and budget support for evaluation have yet to follow. The federal agencies are still severely lacking in evaluative capacity. The GAO reports, for example, in 1993 that major U.S. training programs for dislocated workers such as Trade Adjustment Assistance and Economic

Dislocation and Worker Adjustment Assistance have not been evaluated (U.S. General Accounting Office, 1992). As Havens aptly indicates: "Evaluation capacity will not be created and maintained unless the agency leadership wants that capacity, is prepared to invest in its creation, demands high-quality work, and uses the results of that work" (Havens, 1992). Then, and only then, is it a question of resources.

Program Evaluation at the State Level

State and local governments were slow to follow much of the national-level evaluations of the 1960s and 1970s (Klemanski, 1992). Reasons given for the lack of evaluation are that these levels of government had little of the time, trained personnel, or funding to conduct adequate evaluations of the programs they created, funded, or were to implement. Hatry, Winnie, and Fisk who developed an early guide on practical program evaluation for state and local government officials, spoke of these barriers, as well as the beliefs of many managers that the value of their programs could not be measured and their fear of producing controversy (Hatry, Winnie, and Fisk, 1973).

In 1969 only three states had legislative program evaluation units (Brown, 1988). In 1975 a survey conducted by the Advisory Commission on Intergovernmental Relations found that most state legislatures were ignorant of federal funds coming into the state (Advisory Commission on Intergovernmental Relations, 1981). By 1981, however, thirty-seven states were appropriating federal funds in some degree and fashion. By the early 1980s many states were tracking and analyzing use of federal aid and setting up procedures for an improved legislative role in making decisions related to those funds. This transformation is due in part to states' modernizing their institutions, hiring more highly trained staff, and improving financial management practices as well as improving their revenue systems (U.S. General Accounting Office, 1990).

The transformation was also due to the Reagan administration's philosophy of greatly increasing the states' role in the intergovernmental system by focusing program responsibility on them and of seeking regulatory relief for them. States became more prominent also as federal budgetary retrenchment thrust them into new roles. By the end of the 1980s, the states were the leaders and program innovators in many areas of domestic policy.

State program evaluation increased at the same time as it was decreasing at the federal level. The development of state legislative evaluation units followed the trend. The National Conference of State Legislatures (NCSL), reported in 1992 that forty-five states had established state legislative evaluation units (National Conference of State Legislatures, 1992).

Jones indicates that the state legislative evaluation units generally were modeled after the U.S. General Accounting Office and were designed to provide the legislature with objective, accurate, and independently generated information about state agencies and programs (Jones, 1987). Like the GAO then, these units were established on an accountability model. NCSL (1992) reports:

> Legislatures have used three approaches for organizing program evaluation staff. The two most popular approaches are to create a program evaluation unit within an existing audit agency or to assign program evaluation responsibilities to staff in another legislative staff agency.... The third approach, used by nine states, is to create a separate staff that does only program evaluation.

Evaluation units were not only established as part of the legislative branch of government at the state level. Within the executive, program evaluation was typically made a budget agency function. Again this placement follows an accountability model. Evaluative information could easily tie into budget decisions if the two functions were collocated. As of 1992, forty-four states indicated that program evaluation was a major budget agency function (National Association of State Budget Officers, 1991). For example, in 1979 the governor of the state of Florida created an evaluation and program review unit in the Office of Planning and Budgeting. The evaluation unit is to use a rigorous analytical perspective to review agency budget requests; assess agency effectiveness in meeting program objectives; and develop program performance outcome measures (Polivka and Stryker, 1983).

As of 1992, eleven states reported having a program evaluation function outside the budget agency as part of the responsibility of another executive agency (Polivka and Stryker, 1983). For example, the state of Louisiana established the Bureau of Evaluation in the State Department of Education in 1980. Through the use of objective and systematic methods the Bureau is to assess the extent to which policy and program goals are realized; it is to analyze cost-effectiveness and factors associated with successful and unsuccessful outcomes. It responds to the informational needs of the state legislature, the state board of education, and the state superintendent of education (Peck and Triplett, 1983).

And the evaluation conducted by these state legislative and/or executive evaluation units is often very good. Often mentioned, for example, is Virginia's Department of Planning and Budget's evaluation section which was created in 1983 to conduct program evaluations and special studies for the governor, the governor's secretaries, and the legislature (Mahone and Corbin-Howerton, 1988). The unit conducts studies such as the staffing and treatment in Virginia's mental health hospitals and an evaluation of the tax-exempt status of Blue Cross/Blue Shield's Open Enrollment Health Insurance Program. Those involved with the program believe the units placement in the budget office has been advantageous. As indicated by the above examples, however, these units generally focused on the evaluation of state-funded programs.

Local Level Evaluation Capacity

Evaluation conducted at the local or community level has been a particular challenge. The budget cuts made during the Reagan administration fell most heavily on localities. Federal aid for economic development, housing, and public infrastructure programs, which tended to be federal-state programs, took the brunt of the cuts. Localities did not by and large share in the growth in program evaluation units that states experienced. Still today, many communities lack access to personnel trained in evaluation or cannot support them on a limited government payroll. Often, project staff are asked to perform evaluation as one of many duties, but one for which they may not be well trained. Yet it is in the small towns, suburbs, and major urban centers that federal and state-funded programs and activities are carried out.

In the 1990s, as earlier, federal emphasis has been on providing localities with technical assistance to improve their capability to conduct evaluations to learn whether local programs work. The audience for these evaluations are the localities and not the federal government. For example, in 1991 the Office for Substance Abuse Prevention in the U.S. Department of Health and Human Services funded the development of a workbook to provide program directors, staff, teachers, and community activists the concepts and principles of evaluation so that they could participate in the evaluation process (Linney and Wandersman, 1991).

The introduction to the workbook clearly states the problem it is intended to address:

> Alcohol and other drug problems have become a major priority in our communities. As a result…thousands of prevention programs and activities are being implemented across the country…. Increasingly, these programs need to assess their activities in order to make decisions about allocation of limited resources…Yet, many people who are being asked to do a 'program evaluation' as part of their many tasks feel unprepared to do it. Therefore, there is an urgent need to provide information to school and community personnel on how to document their program and its possible effects. (Linney and Wandersman, 1991, p. 1)

It is also clear from this example, however, that the federal government is not the audience for the local evaluation.

Federal and State Efforts to Use Each Other's Evaluations

When it comes to its program evaluation needs, the federal government has typically relied on third-party evaluation. The executive generally contracts with private research firms for national evaluations of state or local implementation of federal programs. The U.S. Congress frequently, as discussed previously, turns to the GAO. Independence of the evaluation is believed to be key. While the federal government may contract with associations representing states for information collection on state or local practices or opinions, to determine the effectiveness of a federal program, it looks for that independence.

The federal government's accountability orientation has for the most part prevented the type of intergovernmental evaluation discussed earlier in this paper. The selection of the contractor and the general design of the evaluation are decisions made at the federal level. States, or organizations representing them, may be consulted for advice or suggestions. They may be asked to review instrumentation. Such actions in a loose intergovernmental partnership are likely to improve the quality of the study and increase participation in it. But the decision making is clearly at the federal level and the major audience for the resulting report is the federal government.

In fact, the resulting evaluation report may greatly affect the state if the federal government makes resource decisions on the basis of the study and funds are increased or decreased for the program as a whole. But on a practical level, states report that national evaluations do not meet their needs. They do not often help them to improve the state and local programs. Blalock indicates that this situation exists because of the sampling requirements of the large scale national evaluations. They are designed to break results down by key variables but not by state or local program (Blalock, 1993).

What about federal use of state evaluations? As far back as 1976, the federal government funded efforts to determine if state evaluations could be aggregated and a national picture of the program obtained. One such effort occurred in the Migrant Education Program in 1976. At that time, Title I of the Elementary and Secondary Education Act, as amended, provided grants to State Education Agencies to fund programs that met the special educational needs of children of migratory agricultural workers and fishermen. The then U.S. Office of Education (now the Department of Education) contracted with a private firm, Research Triangle Institute, to determine if required State evaluation reports could be summarized to provide a national perspective (Fisher, 1976).

The resulting report indicated that very few strengths could be found in the state evaluations; instead the result was a catalog of weaknesses. The state reports suffered from problems such as: (1) nonrepresentative sampling procedures; (2) the absence of statistical tests; and (3) use of grade equivalent scores rather than standard scores and/or percentiles to evaluate program effects. While Research Triangle Institute was to use the analysis to develop an evaluation handbook that would include appropriate evaluation designs for state and local use, the firm concluded that the state evaluation data could not be summarized across the States in order to obtain a national picture of the program.

Possible Trends

Recently, some states have contracted with private firms for sophisticated evaluations of programs funded at least in part with federal funds. For example, California has a statewide program called Greater Avenues for Independence (GAIN) Program.[5] The program emphasizes participation in basic education as a condition for receiving welfare for those "GAIN determines to need basic education." Federal funding is provided through the Job Opportunities and Basic Skills Training Programs (JOBS) which is the major source of funding for state welfare-to-work programs. JOBS provides competitive grants for demonstration projects; the demonstrations are required to include an evaluation component with an experimental net impact evaluation, among other requirements.

The California Department of Social Services (CDSS) oversees GAIN which is administered by California's fifty-eight counties. CDSS has contracted with the Manpower Demonstration Research Corporation for a random assignment evaluation of GAIN's effectiveness in six of the counties. Additionally, the federal government is providing funding for the collection and analysis of literacy test data (Martinson and Friedlander, 1994).

This evaluation is considered to be relevant to welfare reform at the national level. This is not only because of the size of California's welfare caseload or its experiment with mandating basic education for large numbers of welfare recipients, but also because of the rigorous design of the study to measure the program's effectiveness. Additionally, the evaluation's independence is viewed as assured by the third-party evaluation. This viewing of states as laboratories for social experiments whose lessons can be used nationally—at least as long as third-party rigorous effectiveness evaluations are conducted—may be an emerging trend of the 1990s. Joint federal and state funding of such effectiveness evaluations could become a new model for intergovernmental evaluation.

Conclusion

Historically, intergovernmental evaluation—the joint funding, planning, and conduct of an evaluation by two or more levels of government—has been the exception, not the norm, in the United States. The federal government has been the strong lead in conducting evaluations to determine if the intergovernmental policy or program is successful. Very recently, however, there are signs that the states are becoming full players in the field of program evaluation. In fact, in some areas, states are clearly taking the lead role. While evaluations are not yet intergovernmental—the federal and state governments do not typically jointly sponsor, design, or conduct program evaluations—the action is no longer unilaterally top-down. Instead, the federal government is, in some cases, learning from state evaluations and using them in policymaking. As concerns the local level of government, emphasis is on improving evaluation capacity.

Notes

1. Though the legislation that brings many policies and programs into existence originate at the federal level, the sources of ideas for these policies and programs vary. Ideas for policies and programs may originate with citizens, individual lawmakers and other government officials, or from existing programs already operating at the state or local level. For a general overview of the sources of ideas for programs and policies, see John Kingdon, *Agendas, Alternatives, and Policies*, New York: Harper Collins Publishers, 1994 and Nelson W. Polsby, *Political Innovation in America: The Politics of Policy Initiation*, New Haven, Yale University Press, 1984.
2. In the United States, the federal and state governments fund a variety of programs to assist individuals and families who either have no income or have very low incomes. These programs provide a variety of services such as cash payments to purchase food, financial subsidies for housing, job training, and child care assistance. Each program has its own eligibility criteria. Generally, however, individuals must have an income that is lower that poverty standards established by the federal government.
3. The executive and legislative branches are two of the three major branches of the U.S. national government. The President oversees the executive branch which is comprised of agencies that administer federal laws. Congress, a deliberative and lawmaking body that includes among its responsibilities oversight of federal programs, is the legislative branch. The two branches work closely together to make national policy.
4. Authorizing legislation provides approval for federal expenditure of funds for a given purpose. However, in order for funds to actually be made available, Congress must also enact an appropriations bill that specifies how much money can spent for the program. Without an appropriation, federal funding cannot be made available for the programs implementation. The amount that Congress actually appropriates for a program cannot exceed the amount authorized.
5. California's Greater Avenues for Independence (GAIN) program began in 1985 as a statewide initiative. The federal Job Opportunities and Basic Skills Training (JOBS) Program is modeled on California's GAIN program.

References

Advisory Commission on Inter-governmental Relations (1981). *In Brief: State and Local Roles in the Federal System*. Washington: ACIR.

Blalock, A. (ed.) (1993). "National Research." In *Evaluation Forum*, Issue 9. Washington, DC: U.S. Department of Labor.

Brown, J.R. (1988). "State Evaluation in an Executive Environment." In C.G. Wye and H.P. Hatry, eds. *Timely, Low-Cost Evaluation in the Public Sector*, New Directions for Program Evaluation, 38, 37–47.

Fisher, M. and C. Place (1976). "Summary of Procedures Employed." In *State Evaluation Reports of Title 1 Migrant Programs*. Research Triangle Park, NC: Research Triangle Institute (Project No 224-1235; Contract 300-76-0095).

Hatry, H.P., R.E. Winnie, and D. Fisk (1973). *Practical Program Evaluation for State and Local Government Officials*. Washington, DC: The Urban Institute Press.

Havens, H.S. (1992). "The Erosion of Federal Program Evaluation." In C.G. Wye and R.C. Sonnichsen, eds., *Evaluation in the Federal Government: Changes, Trends, and Opportunities*, New Directions in Program Evaluation, 55, 21–27.

Havens, H.S. (1990). *The Evolution of the General Accounting Office: From Voucher Audits to Program Evaluations*. Washington, DC: U.S. General Accounting Office.

Hyde, A.C. and J.M. Shafritz (1979). *Program Evaluation in the Public Sector*. New York: Praeger Special Studies.

Jones, R. (1987). "Keeping an Eye on State Agencies." In *State Legislatures*. Denver, CO: National Conference of State Legislatures.

Klemanski. J.S. (1992). Book review of *Evaluating Social Programs at the State and Local Level: The JTPA Evaluation Design Project*. In M. F. Smith and Carl Wisler, eds., *Evaluation Practice*, 13/3, 207–08.

Levine, R.A. (1983). "Contractor Evaluation for the Federal Government." In Robert St. Pierre, ed., *Management and Organization of Program Evaluation*, New Directions for Program Evaluation, 18, 67–68.

Linney, J.A. and A. Wandersman (1991). *Prevention Plus III: Assessing Alcohol and Other Drug Prevention Programs at the School and Community Level: A Four-Step Guide to Useful Program Assessment*. Washington, DC: U.S. Department of Health and Human Services, Office for Substance Abuse Prevention, DHHS Publication No. (ADM)91-1817.

Mahone, John A. and Lin Corbin-Howerton (1988). "State Evaluation in an Executive Environment." In C.G. Wye and H.P. Hatry, eds., *Timely, Low-Cost Evaluation in the Public Sector*, New Directions for Program Evaluation, 38, 37–47.

Martinson, K. and D. Friedlander (1994). *GAIN: Basic Education in a Welfare-to-Work Program: Executive Summary*. New York: Manpower Demonstration Research Corporation.

Nathan, Richard P. (1988). *Social Science in Government*. New York: Basic Books.

National Conference of State Legislatures (1992). *The Use of Sunset and Program Evaluation in the State Legislatures: Presentation to the Sunset Review Subcommittee, Indiana Legislative Council*. Denver, CO: National Conference of State Legislatures.

Peck, H.I. and S.E. Triplett (1983). "Management and Organization of an Evaluation Unit in a State Education Agency." In R.G. St. Pierre, ed., *Management and Organization of Program Evaluation*, New Directions for Program Evaluation, 18, 39–47.

Polivka, L. and L.T. Stryker (1983). "Program Evaluation and the Policy Process in State Government: An Effective Linkage." In E. Chelminsky, *Program Evaluation: Patterns and Directions*. Washington, DC: American Society for Public Administration.

Provus, Malcolm (1971). *Discrepancy Evaluation: For Educational Program Improvement and Assessment*. Berkeley, CA: McCutchan Publishing Corporation.

Richardson, E.L. (1992). "The Value of Evaluation." In C.G. Wye and R.C. Sonnichsen, eds., *Evaluation in the Federal Government: Changes, Trends, and Opportunities*, New Directions for Program Evaluation, 55, 15–20.

Rist, R.C. (1990). "The Organization and Function of Evaluation in the United States: A Federal Overview." In Ray C. Rist, ed., *Program Evaluation and Management of Government*, New Brunswick, NJ: Transaction Publishers.

Rossi, P.H. and H.E. Freeman (1982). *Evaluation: A Systematic Approach*. California: Sage Publications.

Trask, R.R. (1991). *GAO History 1921–1991*. Washington, DC: U.S. General Accounting Office, GAO/OP-3-HP.

U.S. General Accounting Office (1992). *Dislocated Workers: Comparison of Assistance Programs*. Washington, DC: U.S. General Accounting Office, GAO/HRD-92-153BR.

U.S. General Accounting Office (1992). *Program Evaluation Issues*. Washington, DC: U. S. General Accounting Office, GAO/OGC-93-6TR.

U.S. General Accounting Office (1990). *Federal-State-Local Relations: Trends of the Past Decade and Emerging Issues*. Washington, DC: U.S. General Accounting Office, GAO/HRD-90-34.

U.S. General Accounting Office (1988). *Program Evaluation Issues*. Washington, DC: U. S. General Accounting Office, GAO/OGC-89-8TR.

U.S. General Accounting Office (1987). *Federal Evaluations: Fewer Units, Reduced Resources, Different Studies from 1980*. Washington, DC: U.S. General Accounting Office, GAO/PEMD-87-9.

Wargo, Michael J. (1983). "Management of the Evaluation Function Within the Federal Government." In Robert G. St. Pierre, ed., *Management and Organization of Program Evaluation*, New Directions for Program Evaluation, 18, 5–25.

Wye, Christopher G. (1992). "The Office of Management and Budget: A Continuing Search for Useful Information." In Christopher G.Wye and Richard C. Sonnichsen, eds., *Evaluation in the Federal Government: Changes, Trends, Opportunities*. New Directions for Program Evaluation, 55, 65–72.

4

Two Cases in Intergovernmental Evaluation in Canada: "Parallel Play" and Cooperation Without Policy Consequences

Robert V. Segsworth and Dale H. Poel

This chapter presents a brief overview of current issues in Canadian federalism and considers the role of formal evaluation in the context of Canadian federalism and Canada's parliamentary system. Two cases in intergovernmental evaluation are given to highlight issues in the implementation and use of program evaluation in this context. The first is an evaluation of an Employment Opportunities Program initiated by the Ontario Ministry of Community and Social Services. The second is the evaluation of the Ontario Legal Aid Plan initiated jointly by the federal Department of Justice and the Ontario Ministry of the Attorney General.

Systemic and Policy Conflict in Canadian Federalism

If one were to read Canada's Constitution Act, one would get the clear impression that Canada is the kind of "classic" federal state that K. C. Wheare discussed in his influential book, *Federal Government* (1946). Article 91 assigns exclusive jurisdiction over a wide range of subjects to the federal government. Article 92 does the same for the provincial governments. Other articles outline areas of concurrent jurisdiction and indicate which level of government has precedence in the event of conflict between federal and provincial policies in those subjects. A residual clause exists to assign jurisdiction for all matters not specifically assigned to provincial governments to the federal government. The Constitution indicates that the federal government may raise revenues by any system of taxation, while provincial governments are limited to direct taxation schemes only.

Careful observation of Canadian federal politics, however, would remove the apparent clarity of two constitutionally "watertight" jurisdictions coexisting in a federal state. The practice of Canadian federalism over the past several decades reflects conflict, cooperation, and competition and a gradual decentralization of power from the national government in Ottawa to the provincial capitals.

Although only two levels of government have constitutional status in Canada, one can easily find at least two additional levels. In the Province of Ontario, for example, metropolitan Toronto constitutes a form of regional government (a regional municipality) and the city of Etobicoke is a classic local government (sometimes referred to as an area municipality). These two levels of government are "creatures" of the provincial government constitutionally, but politically they may be very powerful indeed. For example, the Province of Prince Edward Island elects only four members of the House of Commons; whereas, metropolitan Toronto is represented by approximately thirty-five members of Parliament.

In addition, for some purposes, groupings of provinces are reflected in various ways. In economic development policy for example, the federal government has created the Atlantic Canada Opportunities Agency (ACOA) to assist the four eastern provinces of Newfoundland, Prince Edward Island, Nova Scotia, and New Brunswick. The premiers of the three Maritime provinces meet regularly at the Maritime Premiers Conferences to discuss mutual problems and to develop collective responses to federal-provincial issues when possible. The Newfoundland premier recently is beginning to join this group. Similarly, the Western Economic Diversification Department (WED) is the federal government structure charged with the implementation of regional development policy in the four western provinces of Manitoba, Saskatchewan, Alberta and British Columbia. Western premiers also meet regularly to achieve the same objectives as their counterparts in Atlantic Canada.

In some cases, however, the geographic area affected by federal policies and structures may be subprovincial in size. A classic example exists with FEDNOR, a federal government agency charged with the implementation of federal economic development policy in the northern part of the Province of Ontario. At other times, policy initiatives may involve all levels of government in the country. Shortly after its election to power in 1993, the federal Liberal Government announced a $6 billion infrastructure program. This is an effort to provide an economic stimulus and to reduce high unemployment rates. This new program requires that the federal government provide $2 billion, provincial governments provide $2 billion and municipal and regional government contribute an additional $2 billion in support of approved projects. Although the constitution establishes only two levels of government, the reality is that local governments of various types can and do influence the policies and programs of more senior governments in frequent and meaningful ways.

The practice of federalism is also an ever-changing one. Mallory's (1965) seminal article describes the "five faces" involved in moving from a quasi-unitary state to an increasingly decentralized federation with occasional reversals in the trend. Since World War II, the trend has been one in which the central government has lost power relative to its provincial counterparts.

As this decentralization has occurred, there has been a change in process from "classic" federalism through cooperative federalism to executive federalism (Smiley, 1987). In essence, this involves a decline in legal challenges to the actions of the other level of government and an enhanced process of negotiation and political agreement. It is common practice that first ministers of all provinces meet on a wide range of issues. Federal and provincial ministers responsible for health, finance, agriculture, for example, meet regularly and these political leaders have created a large intergovernmental bureaucracy to support such processes.

During this period, the issues became focused on systemic and policy matters. To some considerable extent, the systemic conflict about the rules of the Canadian constitutional game involved concerns raised by the various governments of Quebec. This province has had a separatist government in the past and has refused to approve the 1982 constitutional amendments. It has seen its demands for constitutional reform remain unfulfilled despite the Meech Lake attempt of the late 1980s and the more recent Charlottetown Accord and this year, 1994, has again voted a separatist party, the Parti Québecois (PQ) into office.

Although Quebec has been concerned historically with preventing federal intrusion into powers assigned to the province by the Constitution, the Meech Lake and Charlottetown Accord experiences provided additional elements of specific interests. In the Meech Lake discussions,

Quebec wanted recognition as a distinct society, increased powers over immigration, a veto on constitutional amendments, and financial compensation when Quebec opts out of national programs (federal-provincial) within provincial jurisdiction. In the Charlottetown negotiations, additional demands emerged. These included federal withdrawal from forestry, mining, tourism, recreation, housing, and municipal and urban affairs areas of jurisdiction, if requested by a province. In addition, jurisdiction over culture and labour market training would become exclusively provincial. The failure of these two initiatives is perceived by many Quebecois as a rejection by the rest of Canada of the legitimate demands of the province for constitutional reform.

In that context, it is not surprising that a new political party, the Bloc Quebecois (BQ), was formed to fight for Quebec sovereignty at the federal level. What is surprising, perhaps, is that support for the BQ within Quebec was so strong that it has formed the Official Opposition in the federal Parliament as a result of the 1993 election.

Western Canadian provinces have also expressed concern regarding the constitutional rules of the game. Their view is that, because of the principle of representation by population, the representation of Western Canadian perspectives on national policies has been weak in the corridors of power in the nation's capital. They have suggested the constitution be amended in such a way that the Senate of Canada, the federal upper house, would become elected, equal, and effective. In other words, they have pressed for equal regional representation in the Senate, election of Senators for limited terms, and much stronger regional representation in the legislative process at the federal level than has existed in the past.

The 1980s were a decade of constitutional reform, constitutional discontent and a failure to accommodate the interest of several provinces by changing the "rules of the game" in Canada. Small wonder, then, that the future of the federation is discussed more seriously and with greater trepidation now than at any time in the past.

Policy Conflict: From Federal Expansionism to Fiscal Restraint

The second area of conflict deals with policy issues and often reflects the reality that the division of powers in the Canadian constitution has not produced "watertight containers." In many ways, this area centers around the matter of "fiscal federalism." Although conditional grants from the federal government to the provinces can be traced as far back as 1927 in the case of old age pensions, they became a very significant factor in Canadian federalism in the post-World War II period.

In the 1950s and 1960s, several federal initiatives involved the creation of national policies which intruded into areas of provincial jurisdiction. One example involved the development of health insurance, medical care coverage and support for postsecondary education. Somewhat later, these three policies were defined as Established Programs Funding (EPF). A second example was that of social assistance for the poor under the Canada Assistance Plan (CAP) which went into effect in 1966. In addition, a variety of regional development initiatives have been implemented. The most recent version is the Economic Regional Development Program (ERDP).

The federal government argues that it has the constitutional right to spend money on anything it wishes. The attractiveness of federal money and the political popularity of such initiatives serve as inducements to provincial governments to "buy in" to the shared cost (conditional grant) programs. Originally, the federal government agreed to provide 50 percent of the costs of such programs operated by the provinces on the condition that the provincial schemes met national standards.

Few provinces resisted despite their complaints that the federal government's initiatives distorted provincial priorities and diverted provincial funds into what Ottawa had determined to be national priorities. Indeed, the Province of Quebec was the only one to "opt-out" in the early stages. Quebec argued that national criteria would not be appropriate for its culturally and linguistically unique population. It agreed, however, to provide similar programs if the federal government would provide the government of Quebec with greater access to taxes levied by the federal government in the province. The federal government agreed and Quebec found itself maintaining at least the appearance of constitutional propriety and achieving greater autonomy from federal controls than did the other provinces.

Dyck (1993) reports that in 1990 there were some 206 multilateral and 193 bilateral federal-provincial programs in place. He notes that federal fiscal transfers to provinces in 1991–92 amounted to some $34.4 billion, exclusive of regional development assistance. By 1993–94, federal fiscal transfers to the provinces had increased to $39.2 billion or approximately 24 percent of total federal government expenditures (*Policy*

Options 1993). In many respects, the issue of federal fiscal transfers to the provinces is the key issue in current discussions of federal-provincial relations in Canada. By the 1970s, the federal government recognized that its conditional grants programs resulted in massive increases in expenditures over which it had little control. As concerns over a growing federal deficit mounted, the federal government took steps to limit and control the rate of growth of its fiscal transfers to the provinces. The recession of the early 1990s raised provincial concerns even higher. The recession reduced the revenue yield from provincial tax sources while demands for certain kinds of services such as health and medical care and social assistance continued to increase. The attempts of the federal government to come to grips with its mounting deficit by cutting fiscal transfers even further placed provincial governments in very difficult straits (De Koven 1993).

Is There a Role for Evaluation?

Canadian federalism is complex, confusing, and in serious trouble. Canada faces the possibility of separation of one of its largest provinces. Financially, deficits are growing at all levels of government. The stakes appear to be even higher than before in discussions and negotiations over existing and new programs and policies which involve more than one level of government.

In this context, one might assume that evaluation would have a useful role to play. It might, for example, identify expensive programs which might be eliminated or suggest programs which could be made more cost-effective. Given the enormous expenditures involved in federal-provincial and other intergovernmental programs in Canada, evaluation might assist in generating significant expenditure reductions and/or improvements to those programs.

There are other reasons to expect that intergovernmental programs would be evaluated in Canada. The original federal evaluation policy which became operative in the early 1980s required that all federal programs be evaluated over a five-year cycle (Segsworth, 1990). Although provincial governments have different policies regarding evaluation, in the case of Ontario, the policy requires that programs whose impact (Segsworth, 1992) is seriously in doubt should be evaluated. The Ontario policy also indicated that in the case of programs that were not likely to be adjusted because of the influence of political pressures, no evaluation should be conducted. In some cases, such as the Economic Regional Development Agreements, there is a requirement that all projects be evaluated and that the evaluation results should feed into a decision process which will terminate and/or renew existing federal-provincial agreements.

There is, however, a great deal in the federal government policy on program evaluation which mitigates against the probability that intergovernmental programs will be subjected to frequent and rigorous evaluations. Federal policy establishes the deputy minister of the department as the client for evaluations and deputy ministers are more likely to be concerned with operational matters. Hartle (1990) for example, argued that fundamental aspects of policy and programs were not evaluated seriously under the federal evaluation policy. The Task Force on Program Review (1985) and the Office of the Comptroller General (1986) noted that the Access to Information Act may have resulted in a tendency by departments to shy away from sensitive issues in conducting evaluation research. Testimony to the Senate Committee on National Finances (Thomas, 1990) by officials of the Department of Fisheries and Oceans indicated that the criteria used to select programs for evaluation were weighted in such a way that senior management needs were weighted equally with the other seven criteria combined. As Segsworth (1993) has pointed out, one of the problems is that federal evaluation policy does not respond to the needs of either Parliament or the public.

The most recent Report of the Auditor General (1993) provides disconcerting evidence of the lack of federal interest and involvement in the evaluation of intergovernmental programs. It notes that "program evaluation has the potential to answer three pressing needs for information":

1. to help make decisions about resource allocation that could contribute to controlling the deficit;
2. to help Canadians determine the value obtained with their tax dollars; and
3. to enable public servants to take responsibility for results rather than process. (p. 219)

The auditor general noted particularly that the more expensive programs were less likely to be subjected to comprehensive evaluations. He found that "with programs such as Post-secondary Education, Fiscal Equalization and Stabilization, and Health Insurance Contributions, new mechanisms involving close consultation and cooperation with provincial governments may need to be developed to ensure that the gaps in evaluation coverage are filled." Indeed, the Auditor General's concern about program evaluation in the Government of Canada reached the point that he suggested that "if the present approach cannot be made to work, Parliament may wish to consider more radical solutions to obtain more timely, relevant and reliable effectiveness information."

It is important to realize that the auditor general's critique of program evaluation is almost entirely from the vantage point of the federal government. This is made clear by the fact that the report was discussed by stakeholders like the federal cabinet, Parliament, central agencies, and federal departments. Utilization is similarly focused on the use of program evaluation by federal actors—Parliament, ministers, deputy ministers, or federal-level program managers. Little emphasis has been placed on intergovernmental collaboration in the evaluation of programs where both levels clearly have interests.

While it is true the large federal program areas such as transfers to the provinces in health insurance and postsecondary education have not been evaluated, smaller subprograms under several shared-cost agreements include requirements for evaluation. For several provinces, the compliance with this requirement for evaluation of subprograms was the first provincial experience with program evaluation. The extension of federal funding for civil legal aid under CAP, for example, was offered to the provinces in the early 1980s with evaluation as one of the conditions for accepting federal funds. The requirements for program evaluation attached to demonstration projects and community-based projects in the fields of crime prevention, programs for seniors, victims services or community health were probably an important transmission line for the diffusion of evaluation practices to provincial and municipal governments in Canada.

A. W. Johnson (1992) concludes that fewer evaluations of larger programs have been implemented because of the important policy, and by definition political, consequences associated with such evaluations in the context of both Canadian federalism and the parliamentary system. Canada has an older institution, the royal commission, that has been used for the review of large national programs and issues of critical political importance. Johnson writes:

> [A] more fundamental problem with the effectiveness evaluation regime as it has developed...is its [lack of] compatibility with the parliamentary system into which

it is being implanted. The essence of that system is that it is political, and adversarial. (p. 26)

Johnson argues that finding alternative strategies for evaluating the more comprehensive policies and programs would leave to the present effectiveness regime the smaller programs, where the political ingredient is small and the administrative ingredient is large.

This line of thinking raises issues that are beyond the scope of this chapter. It is useful, however, to contrast the "larger" from the "smaller" intergovernmental programs and to recognize that most Canadian experience with intergovernmental evaluation has been with the evaluation of the smaller, subprograms of federal-provincial agreements. Our two evaluation cases are "medium-sized" programs, although legal aid is somewhat larger and has a different program status than the demonstration projects found under the Employment Opportunities Program. These two cases demonstrate some of the distinctive features of intergovernmental evaluation in Canada. They reflect the Canadian reality that *highly politicized* policies are *not* normally subject to formal evaluation under existing federal or provincial evaluation and review policies.

Parallel Play: The Employment Opportunities Program (EOP) Evaluation

The Employment Opportunities Program (EOP) was really a series of pilot programs developed by the Ministry of Community and Social Services of Ontario in the early 1980s. The basic aim of each of the programs was to provide services of various kinds to social assistance recipients which would enable these people to find employment and no longer be dependent on welfare. Each program was designed to deal with a specific target group. A profile of each initiative is given in figure 4.1.

The EOP was in many ways an ideal candidate for intergovernmental evaluation. It was reasonably expensive, with a total cost of $42.7 million in 1987–88. Funding for EOP comes from two major sources—the government of Canada and the government of Ontario. Federal funding is provided by the Canada Assistance Plan, a shared-cost program established in 1966. "Under the Canada Assistance Plan (CAP), Ottawa provided half the funding for almost any provincial or municipal program that provided social assistance or welfare services to persons in need" (Dyck, 1993, 363–64). The federal-provincial funding and pro-

Figure 4.1
Employment Opportunities Program Initiatives:
Mandate, Delivery Agent, and Funding Level

Employment Support Initiatives Program	To provide pre-employment counselling for single parents. Delivered by municipal governments throughout the province ($9.9 million in 1987–88)
Youth Employment Program	Provided pre-employment counselling for at least three months to 16–24 year-old youths who had been on social assistance for at least 3 months. Delivered by municipal governments ($1.1 million in 1987–88)
Municipal Job Development Programme	To provide work experience and assist social assistance recipients to find full-time employment. Delivered by municipal governments ($1.3 million annually)
Social Services Employment Porgram	To provide up to 12 months full-time employment in cost-shared CAP agencies for single parents and disabled individuals on welfare. Delivered by provincial Ministry of Community and Social Services ($16.3 million)
Summer Employment Experience Part Time Work Experience	To provide work for 16–20 year-old dependents of social assistance recipients and wards of the Children's Aid Societies during the summer months and during the school year in non-profit community agencies. Delivered by provincial Ministry of Community and Social Services ($4.5 million in 1987–88)
Community Youth Support Program	Provided counselling, case management and referral services for 15–20 year-old youth who were living independently and experiencing difficulty. Delivered by ministry transfer agencies ($4.1 million in 1987–88)
Preparation for Independence Program	Provided life skills and pre-employment training for 15–20 year-old youth. Delivered by ministry transfer agencies ($2.4 million)
Future Residential Component	Provided housing assistance and support to 16–24 year-old youth enrolled in the Futures Program. Delivered by ministry transfer agencies ($3.1 annually)

grams relationship here could be described as multilateral interaction that is unified by the broad federally-created CAP framework, although the decision to evaluate was unilateral. The EOP involved some activities which overlapped potentially with programs operated by the federal government's Employment and Immigration Department. In addition, the delivery mechanisms required the participation of municipal governments, the provincial Ministry of Community and Social Services and a variety of social service agencies.

The EOP evaluation was an expensive one conducted in the period from 1984–1986. Thirteen different studies were completed which attempted to examine both effectiveness and program delivery issues. One of the studies involved a further follow-up of the clients of one evaluation study (Employment Support Initiative). Another provided a literature review of studies related to the evaluation of employment programs for social assistance recipients. The total cost of the evaluation was in excess of $1 million.

The decision to evaluate the EOP resulted initially from a meeting in the hall between a program manager and a member of the Ministry's program evaluation staff. The evaluator suggested that pilot projects such as EOP should be evaluated and the manager agreed. This recommendation was accepted by senior executives within the Ministry.

The provincial ministry also decided that there would be no involvement of the federal government, municipal government, and other delivery agencies in the design and management of the evaluation studies. Stakeholders other than the Ministry of Community and Social Services were expressly excluded despite contrary recommendations from evaluation staff in the Ministry. The decision by senior management reflected political-bureaucratic interests and the fact that the funding for the study was coming exclusively from the Ministry's budget.

Two committees were formed to develop the design of the evaluation project and to oversee the evaluation process. The advisory committee consisted of the assistant deputy minister, senior officials of the ministry and area office program staff. The working committee contained program managers from head office and evaluation staff from the ministry. This group met frequently to develop the terms of reference for the evaluation studies. Their recommendations were approved subsequently by the advisory committee. The advisory committee met rarely to deal with specific concerns expressed by the working committee and to approve requests for additional funding when that was needed. Given the fact that all of the people involved in the design of the evaluation study were from the Ministry, it comes as no surprise that there was little disagreement regarding what the fundamental evaluation questions and the scope of the studies should be. In other words, the evaluators limited themselves to matters of concern to the Ministry of Community and Social Services. Issues such as the possible overlap or complementarity with programs offered by Employment and Immigration Canada were ignored.

Once the working committee had developed the terms of reference for the several evaluations, requests for proposals were issued and external consultants were invited to submit their proposals. The consultants engaged to complete the studies worked closely with the working group. Meetings were common. It should be noted that the consultants did not have access to federal data bases or to most provincial data bases that might have been of some value because of confidentiality provisions of federal and provincial legislation. The participants of the programs being evaluated were asked to sign releases and they, together with program staff, provided most of the information necessary to complete the studies.

Once completed, the evaluation reports were sent to ministry officials, all of the delivery agencies, municipal governments, and the federal government Employment and Immigration and Health and Welfare Departments. The reports generated considerable interest in some jurisdictions, particularly the Western Canadian provinces.

In spite of the intergovernmental character of the program, the variety of funding sources and the rather substantial cost of the program, little in the way of instrumental utilization of the evaluation findings took place. Many of the studies found that programs were largely ineffective. This was particularly true of the programs designed for youth. Naturally, there was some reaction against such findings by individuals and groups which had vested interests in the continuation of these programs. In the end, they succeeded and, for the most part, these ineffective programs continued to operate. One reason suggested for this failure of senior officials to respond is that of frequent turnover of executives within the Ministry. Shortly after they are briefed on the evaluation findings and determine that indeed the problems continue to plague these programs, they are promoted or transferred to other responsibilities. The result is that they do not make the key decisions to terminate or dramatically modify the initiatives.

In addition, there appears to have been little in the way of more indirect utilization. The federal government, for example, has not used the reports to argue that the province is not using federal transfers effectively. The province has not used the reports to feed into its ongoing debate with the federal government regarding the cutbacks in federal transfers to Ontario under the CAP. The federal government, then, has not fielded its own evaluation and has not participated directly in the monitoring of these programs. The evaluation context could not be described as competitive between the levels of government.

Cooperation without Policy Consequences: The Evaluation of Legal Aid in Ontario

Unlike the previous case, the decision to conduct an evaluation of the Ontario Legal Aid Plan (OLAP) was taken in the context of a national evaluation framework (Poel 1993). In the early 1980s the federal Department of Justice received cabinet-level approval for the evaluation of federally supported legal aid services administered by the ten Canadian provinces. The implementation of that mandate required provincial-level cooperation and Nova Scotia was the first province to participate (Poel, Aucoin, and Conway 1980; Poel 1983). This initiative was followed by federal-provincial collaboration in New Brunswick, British Columbia, Manitoba, Saskatchewan, and Alberta. The OLAP and Ministry of the Attorney General in Ontario finally joined this evaluation series in an agreement reached in 1988 (See ABT, 1991).

By 1988, then, the Justice Bureau of Review had acquired considerable experience in the evaluation of legal aid services and had a commitment to an evaluation framework that had been implemented in all Canadian provinces except the two smallest (Prince Edward Island and Newfoundland) and the largest (Ontario). This framework had focused on evaluation questions of access to and the quality and costs of legal aid services.

Federal-provincial relations are more complex in the policy area of justice and the delivery of legal aid services than for the field of job training and employment support. The Ontario EOP programs could be implemented (and evaluated) without significant reference to counterpart programs provided in Ontario by federal-level funding. While the provinces have constitutional responsibility for the administration of justice (including the administration of legal aid services), the criminal law and several other important statutes (e.g., food and drugs, divorce) are federal statutes. In addition, the justices of the provincial supreme courts are federal appointments, while the lower criminal and family court judges are provincial appointments. The intermingling of constitutional responsibilities in justice is an obvious pressure towards cooperation in policy, programs, and evaluation.

The first federal-provincial agreements to cost-share the delivery of criminal legal aid were more generous than social programs funded under CAP, with the federal government paying up to 90 percent of criminal legal aid services. The primary national standards required by the federal government of the provincial plans were in the areas of coverage and client eligibility. The choice of delivery mechanism is left to the provinces and the provinces may require a recipient of legal aid to contribute toward the cost of the service. Within the federal-provincial interaction, the federal policy regarding access and services is a constant across the ten provinces, with variations resulting from areas in which the provinces have discretion—either in terms of how to deliver the services or, in the more affluent provinces, the delivery of additional services beyond the federal requirements.

For a number of reasons, Ontario Ministry officials and OLAP senior managers were concerned the Federal Department of Justice might use the evaluation findings to argue for a change in how the legal aid services were delivered—a change from Ontario's predominantly judicare system in which legal aid services are provided by members of the private bar to clients who have received a certificate for services to a staff lawyer system in which legal aid services are provided to eligible clients by lawyers employed by the legal aid plan. The key issues in the debate over these two approaches to legal aid are their relative costs, the principal of choice of counsel, and quality of services.

The evaluation design, as negotiated between the federal and provincial collaborators, was limited to the judicare or certificate component of OLAP and excluded the staff lawyer components of the plan found in OLAP's specialized community clinics and in its research division. Also, questions of "costing" were limited to a cost forecasting model that operated within the existing parameters of the certificate-based services. The lower level of government, then, was able to negotiate some evaluation questions out of the evaluation design. The final report is organized primarily around federal evaluation priorities that include accessibility, quality of service, financial and costing analysis, and management analysis.

The overall cost of the Ontario evaluation was just under $500,000. In most of the other provinces the federal Department, through its Bureau of Review, paid most of the costs of the contracts with consultants to field the evaluations. The provinces contributed mostly through contributions in kind (staff time, facilities) or absorbed actual expenses in their existing operating budgets. In comparison to the other provinces, Ontario probably contributed a larger portion of the actual evaluation budget (except Quebec which proceeded on its own without federal cooperation). The evaluation costs were relatively low in relationship to the OLAP's budget which was over $114 million in 1987–88 and increased dramatically ($271.5 million for 1991–92) because of the impact of a court decision (R. v. Askov), new refugee determination procedures, increase in the number of prosecutions relating to wife assault, drug and impaired driving offenses.

The negotiations leading up to this evaluation agreement and the final planning of the evaluation were dominated primarily by professional stakeholders. The key stakeholders represented were evaluation professionals from the federal Department of Justice, professionals from the Ontario Ministry of the Attorney General and the OLAP, and representatives of the Law Society of Upper Canada (the legal professions association) which administers the plan for the province and contributes financially to its operation. The stakeholders represented major organizations with considerable continuity and autonomy. In most other provinces the federal level could dominate the evaluation process because it was the major funding source and the primary source of evaluation expertise. This was probably less so in Ontario because of the resources, financial and human, of the provincial government and the relevant departments and agencies.

Politicians as politicians, however, were not significant in the evaluation process. It is interesting that, during the time of this evaluation, three different provincial governments were in power—first the Progressive Conservatives, followed by a Liberal government, and finally a government formed by a social democratic party, the New Democratic Party (NDP). The NDP government was in power when the final evaluation report was available. For some time, the new government was virtually unaware of the evaluation report (personal interview) at the same time as, for reasons of financial restraint, it began pressing for changes in the system towards the staff lawyer model (Onyshko, 1991). A changing political environment can be a greater problem in intergovernmental evaluations where a change in government can create a "new partner" to the evaluation exercise, a partner who may or may not continue the previous commitment to an evaluation in process.

The extent to which a changing political environment influences an evaluation process or the use of its findings will depend, in large part, on whether the evaluation process or findings are of any interest or use to politicians or whether they are primarily the domain of middle and senior managers. In this particular case, the evaluation of OLAP seems less politicized at the federal level and, potentially, of more political use at the provincial level (except the evaluation design did not provide specific information necessary to support changes in the administration of the plan being considered by the new NDP government.)

In contrast to the findings of the EOP evaluation, the overall tone of the Abt report was favorable as reflected in this conclusion:

> Taken together, the data collected for this review present a generally positive picture of the Plan's performance. The Plan is operating a generally accessible service. Both the administration of the Plan and the criteria employed to assess the financial eligibility of applicants are under review. The Plan has also become aware of, and responsive to, the needs of a number of segments of its client population requiring specialized attention.

The Plan should be commended for its accomplishments to date, and encouraged to build on these successes in the future (Abt, 1991: 283).

The report's recommendations suggested ways to improve the administrative efficiency of the Plan and the quality of services. It recommended a restructuring of its organization into a regional design and suggested public information campaigns for several client and referral groups. Most of the recommendations were focused on the management of the legal aid program, not the politics. The report was prevented from saying anything directly about expanding or contracting the staff lawyer services of the plan and said virtually nothing about providing fewer services. As a result, the evaluation report was largely irrelevant to the agenda of the new NDP government which very quickly acquired a myopic focus on budget cuts.

The program questions addressed in the evaluation, then, were important questions for the fine-tuning of a large organization whose management capabilities had lagged behind its program growth. The questions were not immediately part of the provincial or federal political agenda when, after a three-year research effort, the evaluation questions were finally answered. It was not a "rapid feedback" evaluation exercise.

During and following the evaluation period, both levels of government made significant decisions about the funding or delivery of legal aid with little reference to the ongoing evaluation exercise or its conclusions. The federal government responded to double-digit increases in legal aid expenditures during this period (averaging 19 percent/year in Ontario) by placing a cap on its contribution to programs in Ontario, Alberta, and British Columbia—Canada's three wealthiest provinces. The NDP provincial government pressed ahead with its interest in the major alternative delivery system, staff lawyer clinics, and delayed scheduled increases to the tariff schedule which determines the fees paid to private lawyers providing services to certificate clients. The Abt report did not deal with staff lawyer questions and recommended improvements in the fees paid to lawyers.

Applications for Intergovernmental Evaluation

The IIAS Working Group on Policy and Programs Evaluation has concluded in its discussions that the most typical feature of intergovernmental evaluation situations is probably the fact that they contain a large part of the political ingredient. This seems not to be the case in Canada, generally, and especially not in our two cases. The cases used in this chapter, rather, reflect the Canadian reality that "highly politicized" policies and programs are not normally subject to formal evaluation under existing federal or provincial evaluation and review policies. Possible explanations for this may be (1) the focus of evaluation use on program management, an instrumental use suggested in the introductory chapter as the norm for single government evaluation; (2) the setting of the evaluation agenda for Canadian intergovernmental programs largely by the federal level of government where the multilateral programs are unified; and (3) the use of alternative review mechanisms (task forces and Royal Commission) for policy and programs reviews involving major political issues.

The editors define intergovernmental evaluation as a process in which two or more levels of government are involved at one or more stages of the evaluation process, that is, from decision to evaluate to utilization.

This definition is problematic because it leaves a void in Canadian practice. In the case of EOP, a significant share of the program funding came from the federal government, but the programs were created and administered by the Government of Ontario. The evaluation of EOP was undertaken unilaterally by Ontario with no federal involvement, although at some time, results of this evaluation may play a role in federal-provincial discussions of the Canada Assistance Plan.

The definition also ignores situations of policy competition between two levels of government. For example, in the case of Northern Ontario, the Ontario Heritage Fund (provincial government) and FEDNOR (federal government) have virtually identical mandates for the same geographic area and compete with each other. A recent evaluation of FEDNOR noted clients rated FEDNOR as a more efficient vehicle to support their attempts at economic diversification for the region than the Heritage Fund.

These examples illustrate a potential grey area in our understanding of intergovernmental policy and its evaluation. In the first case, even though the policy is "intergovernmental," at least in part, the evaluation was not. In the FEDNOR example, by the definitions of the editors, neither the policies nor the evaluations are intergovernmental. At the same time, these policies reflect federal, provincial and regional interrelationships from an intergovernmental perspective. By not viewing these evaluations from an intergovernmental perspective, certain understandings may be lost such as:

• The failure of existing evaluation policy and/or practice to meet the needs of accountability. In the case of EOP, the federal government seems unconcerned about the effective use of its financial contribution. In the FEDNOR example, the evaluation ignored the issues of duplication, client and citizens confusion, and competition between the federal and provincial programs.

• The failure to ensure adequate and broadly useful evaluation coverage of intergovernmental policies and programs. By applying the narrower definition of the introduction, only one of the two cases examined in this chapter would constitute an intergovernmental evaluation—that is, the evaluation of OLAP. The EOP case would be viewed simply as evaluation by a single level of government. Such a perspective misses the complexity, subtlety, and reality of the dynamics of intergovernmental politics and policies in Canada.

In essence, the issue is whether the evaluation process and the policy being evaluated must be intergovernmental, whether the evaluation process must be "intergovernmental," or the policy or program being evaluated must be "intergovernmental." From our vantage point, the last alternative is the most useful. It would include both the OLAP and the EOP evaluation initiatives.

The OLAP evaluation findings and the Ontario NDP government initiatives in spite of the Abt report may conform to A. W. Johnson's analysis noted above; that is, effectiveness evaluation may not be compatible with the politics of the parliamentary system and, as a result, will be used primarily for management purposes. Two of the most political decisions the Ontario government could take were a decision to pay private lawyers less money for providing legal aid services by delaying fee increases and a decision to press ahead exploring the staff lawyer alternative to the judicare model for delivering legal aid services. They did both and without reference to the evaluation findings. The actual use of the OLAP evaluation report has been for program management, not for policy and political decision making. Ontario received several suggestions for administrative improvements and restructuring. The Federal government found recommendations for change in areas of access and program awareness and received assurances that "overall" the Plan was providing a reasonably good quality service in exchange for its financial contribution.

The use of the Employment Opportunity Program evaluations was potentially very political, given the generally negative findings concerning program impact. In this case, however, the tight control of participants in the evaluation process meant that conflict could be avoided. EOP did not have to respond to findings of ineffectiveness nor to charges of duplication with parallel federal programs. The evaluation circle was drawn close (a single level) and excluded stakeholders from other levels of government who could have used the evaluation findings to criticize the EOP.

The recent report by the Canadian Auditor General (1993) showed that the primary use of federal evaluations was for program understanding and program modification. Program reform was a distance third and program termination was an infrequently used fourth use. Program understanding and modification are not trivial uses and can represent an immediate, as well as longer-term use. The Ontario evaluation experience and its report, for example, showed regionally unequal patterns of access to legal aid to which the Plan could be respond. It also contributed to the larger body of knowledge concerning Canadian legal aid services found in the series of evaluation reports that began with the Nova Scotia evaluation.

The possible areas of serious reform in OLAP or the actual termination of EOP initiatives would be less likely evaluation uses given the evaluation and political context of the two programs. In an intergovernmental context, then, it seems unlikely that evaluation findings in and of themselves will support program decision-making that represents significant reform of the programs.

To some extent both of our evaluation cases fit the "managerial model" of intergovernmental evaluation as discussed in the introductory chapter. The question, however, is more managerial than the one posed by Toulemonde and Rieper whose central question is as follows: "to what extent is the intergovernmental policy or program a successful one?" The question can be reshaped somewhat by adding: "and where can we modify our basically good program to improve it?"

That was the direction of the OLAP evaluation and those in the other provinces, as well. There were different priorities in the several provinces and changes in emphasis over the ten-year time period in which the evaluations were completed. The presence of the federal government as a key actor in each legal aid evaluation, however, brought with it some standardization of design that produced cross-provincial comparability of findings on key factors of access, quality of services, and efficiency.

The series of legal aid evaluations also represent a certain amount of societal learning. Although conflict existed over some issues, there was and is a general consensus that some form of legal aid service must be provided with the Canadian justice system. In that sense, the several professional issues in this field represent only modest levels of conflict. And, the evaluations were certainly focused beyond the narrow question of success or failure. The status of legal aid programs as "required" within the Canadian justice system makes them significantly different than the EOP programs that existed as provisional, "pilot" projects.

The status of programs must have a significant bearing on intergovernmental evaluations. Comparisons between the two cases in this regard may have been less clear, however, because of the limited intergovernmental involvement in the EOP evaluation. Its evaluation profile is significantly different than for OLAP. In the EOP evaluation the provincial level controlled all the activities, except for the use of findings. This evaluation profile made reaching consensus on the evaluation design easier and allowed the evaluation to ignore some important questions of overlap with alternative federal programs. In the OLAP evaluation, most evaluation activities were shared by both levels, with federal contributions dominant in only a few agenda items and in funding. The OLAP evaluation design narrowed the scope of the research, but the conclusion resulted from tough negotiations.

The discussion of the "accountability" model seems misdirected in the parliamentary system of Canada where the government is accountable to Parliament (or the provincial legislative assemblies), rather than directly to society. That is the basic distinction between responsible and representative government. The fact that the EOP evaluation could find the programs largely ineffective and yet have the evaluation findings ignored by everyone suggests there was no political advantage to the opposition parties in picking up the issue. Similarly, the fine-tuning suggested by the legal aid evaluation was of interest to the civil servants/lawyers managing the Plan, but not the opposition parties or citizens, in general.

Evaluation Policy in Canada without Formal Reference to IGE

The relationship between program evaluation and accountability as discussed by A. W. Johnson (1992) highlights the current disagreements in Canada about the place and use of program evaluation before Parliament. We accept his suggestion, discussed above, that the political context of Parliament makes it difficult to use any evaluation for comprehensive policy review, intergovernmental or not. Similarly, contexts in which intergovernmental relations involve questions of policy or politics are probably contexts where program evaluations, at best, can provide background information or, at worst, be misappropriated for the politics of the day.

In May 1994, the government of Canada approved a new policy on program review, internal audits and evaluation (Treasury Board, 1994). In the context of intergovernmental evaluation, this new policy is more interesting for what it does *not* include. Perhaps in response to the concerns expressed by the auditor general, the new policy emphasizes a need and responsibility for the Treasury Board Secretariat to coordinate or conduct "occasional reviews addressing multi-departmental and government-wide issues." The new policy, however, says nothing about the review or evaluation of intergovernmental policies and programs. It reflects what our case studies have illustrated:

• Federal and provincial government evaluation policies do not include formal provisions for the evaluation of intergovernmental policies and programs.

• Because existing evaluation policies have the deputy head (senior bureaucrat) as the client for the vast majority of evaluations, most evaluation studies reflect managerial rather than policy concerns.

• Intergovernmental evaluations, when they exist, reflect ad hoc agreements on what to evaluate, what evaluation questions are to be posed, how the studies should be conducted and who should be involved in the evaluation process.

• Major intergovernmental programs and policies are *not* subjected to evaluations under existing federal and provincial evaluations.

This revised federal policy reflects the tremendous political sensitivity of the Government of Canada to the dynamics of federalism and the political difficulties of unilaterally engaging in formal evaluations of major federal-provincial programs.

References

Auditor General of Canada (1993). *Annual Report.* Ottawa: Supply and Services.

Abt Associates of Canada (1991). *Comprehensive Review and Evaluation of the Certificate Component of the Ontario Legal Aid Plan.* Prepared for the Ontario Ministry of the Attorney General and the Federal Department of Justice.

Comptroller General of Canada (1986). *The Effects of the Access to Information Legislation on the Program Evaluation Function.* Ottawa: Program Evaluation Branch, Office of the Comptroller General of Canada.

De Koven, Harriet L. (1993). "Federal-Provincial Transfers: Which Way From Here?" *Policy Options,* vol. 14, no. 10, pp. 45–48.

Dyck, Rand (1993). *Canadian Politics: Critical Approaches.* Scarborough: Nelson Publishers.

Hartle, D. (1990). "Increasing Government Accountability: A Proposal that the Senate Assume Responsibility for Program Evaluation." *Proceedings of the Standing Committee on National Finance.* 3 May, Appendix NF-23a.

Johnson, A.W. (1992). "Reflections on Administrative Reform in the Government of Canada, 1962–1991: A Discussion Paper." Prepared for Office of the Auditor General, Ottawa.

Mallory, J. (1965). "The Five Faces of Canadian Federalism." In P.A. Crepeau and C.B. Macpherson, eds., *The Future of Canadian Federalism.* Toronto: University of Toronto Press.

Onyshko, T. (1991). "Secret paper shows public defender system considered." *The Lawyers Weekly* (December 13, p. 9).

Poel, D.H., P. Aucoin, and R. Conway (1980). *Nova Scotia Legal Aid: A Review and Proposal for Evaluation*. Halifax: The Nova Scotia Legal Aid Commission and Federal Department of Justice.

Poel, D.H. (1983). *The Nova Scotia Legal Aid Evaluation Report: Entering the "Third Generation."* Halifax: The Nova Scotia Legal Aid Commission and the Federal Department of Justice.

Poel, D.H. (1993). "Cooperation and Conflict in the Evaluation of Legal Aid Services in the Canadian Provinces." In J. Hudson and J. Roberts, eds., *Evaluating Justice: Canadian Policies and Programs*. Toronto: Thompson Educational Publishing, Inc., 1993.

Policy Options (1993). *Fiscal Federalism: Debating Canada's Future* (vol. 14, no.10). Montreal: Institute for Research and Public Policy.

Segsworth, R.V. (1990). "Policy and Program Evaluation in the Government of Canada." In R.C. Rist, ed., *Program Evaluation and the Management of Government*. New Brunswick, N.J.: Transaction Publishers.

Segsworth, R.V. (1992). "Governmental Activity Review in Ontario." In J. Hudson, J. Mayne, and R. Thomlinson, eds. *Action-Oriented Evaluation*. Toronto: Emerson and Wall.

Segsworth, R.V. (1993). "Public Access to Evaluation in Canada." In R. Conner, J. Hudson, J. Mayne, and M. L. Bemelmans-Videc, eds., *Advancing Public Policy Evaluation*. Amsterdam: North Holland.

Smiley, D. (1987). *The Federal Condition in Canada*. Toronto: McGraw Hill Ryerson Limited.

Task Force on Program Review (1985). *Introduction to the Process of Program Review*. Ottawa: Supply and Services.

Thomas, J.F. (1990). "Opening Statement." *Proceedings of the Senate Standing Committee on National Finance on 17 May*. Ottawa.

Treasury Board (1994). *Treasury Board Manual on Review, Internal Audit and Evaluation*. Ottawa: Treasury Board Secretariat.

Wheare, K.C. (1946). *Federal Government*. London: Oxford University Press.

5

Intergovernmental Evaluation of an EU-Funded Regional Development Program in Denmark

Olaf Rieper

The Nordtek Program and its Context

A widespread interest in, and optimistic attitude towards, the promises of new information technology as a means of enhancing regional development swept over the Western world and culminated in the mid 1980s. In particular the use of the new information technology seemed promising as a means of building communication networks in and between local communities in peripheral areas. The new information technology was used directly to link economic growth and local development, in France as part of a huge technological and industrial program, and in the Nordic countries as an element of revitalization of rural areas. These efforts were often given the form of social field experiments (Rieper, Blais and Larsen, 1988). In general it was a widespread assumption, if not a belief, that new information technology, especially telematics, could contribute to the development of peripheral regions all over the industrialized world (Heide, 1990).

In Denmark a number of regional development programs were launched from 1985 to 1990. The means of stimulating regional development in these programs were different kinds of support for the use of new information technology in small and medium-sized enterprises. These included advisory services for new information technology, training packages in new information technology for principals and employees as well as for the unemployed, and common facilities of new information technology to be shared by several small and medium-sized enterprises.

Most of these programs were established primarily because the increased use of new information technology was expected to have a positive impact on the economic activity of the region, and because the counties would be able to get financial support from the European Regional Development Fund (ERDF) as well as from the Danish government. The counties which were eligible for support from ERDF were the so-called less favored areas with relatively high rates of unemployment, a high share of agriculture and fishing industry, and many small and medium-sized enterprises across different industries. At present, the size of these programs varies from approximately 1 million ecus to approximately 35 million ecus. The duration of the programs varies from three to five years.

The program theory for this effort can be summarized as follows. There is a lower degree of utilization of new information technology in small and medium-sized enterprises in the peripheral areas due to the characteristics of these firms and the generally low awareness and knowledge of the potential of new information technology. The manager involved in the day-to-day operations does not have the time to search and digest information about new information technology. Often the small and medium-sized enterprises have a short planning horizon and a low degree of formalization of procedures in the firm's administration and production, which are factors that hamper the implementation of new information technology. As for the peripheral areas in general, it is well known that the diffusion of new technology occurs there later than in the metropolitan areas. This is probably due to several factors such as lower level of education, lower share of high technology enterprises and lower share of services. Therefore, one of the programs' aims was to introduce various kinds of technological services in the local community itself in order to stimulate a faster, better use of new information. It is believed, moreover, that such technological development will have a beneficial impact on the productivity, flexibility and innovative capacity of the small and medium-sized enterprises. Thus, the programs are seen as an important means of raising the level of employment in the areas concerned (Rieper, 1991).

As mentioned in the subsequent chapter on subsidiarity by Jacques Toulemonde, the European Regional Policy is jointly implemented by European, national, and regional levels of government in a partnership approach. This approach involves bilateral co-operation between the Commission and the authorities in the member states as part of co-programming and co-financing activities, formalized in bilateral contracts (Community Support Framework and Monitoring Committees). This implies that the European regional programs are very different from one region to another. The relations between the European and regional level concerning a specific program are much shaped by the nationally shaped relations between the national and regional level of government.

In Denmark, the regions (with the counties as the regional governments) and the local level (with the municipalities as the local governments) have been very much aware of the possibility of funding for regional and local development.[1] Several of the Danish regions were eligible for support from the ERDF, and this opportunity was welcomed by a number of Danish counties, which also wanted to stress the role of the counties in regional business development.[2] The counties are the middle level of government in Denmark. Their main functions are as providers of health services, secondary education, social welfare of the disabled, regional planning, environmental protection and the construction and maintenance of motorways and public transport.

Denmark is divided into fourteen counties and 275 local authorities (municipalities). Both levels have their own elected councils and own taxation base. The local level of government (the municipalities) is more influential than the regional level (the counties). The municipalities have a larger tax base (DKK 91 million) than the counties (DKK 36 million), and they perform more tasks than the counties.

Danish local governments have a long, strong tradition of autonomy within a unitary state and, apart from their statutory functions, have a general competence to act within their geographical boundaries. Interaction between the local levels of government and the national government is shaped by the multilateral relations between the national associations of the local governments and the national government.

The NordTek Program: First, Soft, Decentralized, and Multilevel

The initiative to launch the program came from the region itself stimulated by the options of having ERDF funding and the possibility of obtaining supplementary funding from different sources. The program was formulated by the planning department in the county of North Jutland in cooperation with the municipalities, business development boards, the regional based university, other regional associations, and the national authorities.

The NordTek Programs served as a model for future EU regional programs in that for the first time in the European Community the ERDF program format was used instead of its project format. Also funding from the ERDF was integrated with funding from the EU Social Fund, another EU structural fund. In Denmark NordTek was the first ERDF-funded regional development program. Thus, there was considerable interest in the outcome of the program.

The North Jutland Technology Program (NordTek) was launched in January 1987 and was concluded at the end of 1991. The ultimate aim of the program was to increase employment in North Jutland and get rid of the region's status as "peripheral region" through the well-planned introduction of new technology. The program was intended particularly to increase the use of information technology among the region's small and medium-sized companies.

The total public and private sector funding of the NordTek Program amounted to 35 million ecus including 10 million ecus from the European Regional Development Fund and 8 million ecus from the county of North Jutland. The remainder was in the form of other public and municipal grants and payments by users. In addition, the European Social Fund made a grant of 8 million ecus for the period 1989–91 for various education projects (a so-called integrated scheme).

The program was administered by a bottom-up approach. The operational projects were formulated by local units (e.g. municipality, company, educational center) and applications were sent to the program administration at the regional level for approval. More than 100 projects were financed under the NordTek Program.

The allocation of the program's funding was steered by a committee of twenty-two members representing the county, regional organizations and associations, ministries and the EU. Three levels of government were directly involved, with the regional level holding the majority in membership. The municipalities were indirectly represented through the regional development board. The mayor of the county was head of the committee, signaling the political importance of the program. The operational decisions were de facto taken by the board consisting of members from the county administration, the minister of commerce and trade represented by the regional development department, the University of Aalborg (AUC), the Technological Information Center which is part of a national technological service center, and two regional organizations. The chairman of the board was the chief executive of the county. Three levels of government were involved, in that the municipalities were indirectly represented. The EU level was not represented on the board.

The composition of the steering committee reflects the main influences of the regional level on the allocation of the program's resources, the national and the EU level being more in the background. The high degree of autonomy at the project level is illustrated by the independent operations of the projects under the program, once they had been approved. However, the program administration monitored the projects while in operation. Often the municipalities were represented on the boards of the projects.

The evaluators were thus faced with a multilevel steered program involving two or more levels of government as noted in figure 5.1.

The program consisted of about 100 projects of which 75 percent were directed towards the small and medium enterprises. Most of the projects offered educational and advisory services to companies, access to advanced computer facilities, etc. Thus, the NordTek Program was primarily a "soft" program in contrast to the "hard" programs aiming at improving the physical infrastructure. This has consequences for the evaluation because the outcome of the "soft" programs is more difficult to trace than the outcome of a "hard" program where indicators are more visible and more easily available, such as kilometers of motorway constructed or number of trees planted, or water pollution treatment plants constructed.

The Evaluation of the NordTek Program

Figure 5.1 indicated that mainly two levels of government—the regional and the national—were involved in the evaluation. In practice, however, the local as well as the EU level were also involved, but to a lesser degree.

In this chapter the various stages of the evaluation process are described, focusing on the intergovernmental character of the evaluation. We show how the various levels have shaped the evaluation at various stages, and how the evaluator has coped with problems and challenges raised by the intergovernmental character of the evaluation.[3]

Figure 5.1
The Steering Profile of the Program—Main Actors involved at Various
Stages of the Program

	EU	National	Regional	Local
Legal	F	F	F	
Funding	S	S	S	(S)
Aim and strategy	S	(S)	S	
Implementation			F	F
Monitoring		S	S	
Evaluation		S	S	(S)

F: responsibility, each level has its own legal norms
S: shared responsibility
( ): less important

Evaluation of the NordTek Program was not compulsory at any governmental level under the laws and regulations in force when the program was launched. However, there was a growing interest in evaluation in the Danish Ministry of Industry and Trade, and after the reform of the ERDF, external program evaluation was to become compulsory, and a condition for further funding.

In a broad sense, the wave of evaluation research hit Denmark in the mid 1980s (Rist, 1990) and the awareness of the potential constructive role of evaluation was increasing at all levels of government. At that time, however, the administrative and political culture in Denmark had not yet integrated evaluation research as a tool in the management of programs nor in the development of policy. There was no shared understanding of the benefits of evaluations. The professionalization of evaluation researchers was still incipient. For example, the first Danish book on evaluation methods was published in 1986 by AKF, a Danish research institute.

Civil servants from the planning department of the county of North Jutland had close contacts with the Commission in Brussels and knew that evaluation of the ERDF-funded programs would be compulsory in the future. They encouraged the steering committee of the NordTek Program to fund an evaluation from program resources. It was anticipated that 0.5–1 percent of the program's budget would be used for this purpose. The decision to evaluate and the choice of the evaluator (AKF) was approved by the steering committee. In theory three levels of government were involved, but in practice the decision was prepared by the program director in interaction with the chairman of the board and the chairman of the steering committee, both at the regional level.

The evaluation questions were to be limited to some of the NordTek's intermediary aims: it would be impossible to evaluate the program's final aim (increasing the level of employment in North Jutland) before the program came to an end, since any impact on the region's level of employment would not have materialized by that stage. Therefore, the evaluation should focus on intermediary aims relating to two of the program's main objectives. The first was to strengthen areas in the business structure where industrial environments could be built on the basis of strong positions within a market or by use of new technology, in particular information technology. The second objective was to improve the qualifications of the workforce by promoting knowledge of the new technologies.

The evaluation questions agreed by the program director and AKF were to investigate the extent to which the NordTek Program had contributed to:

- the introduction and utilization of new technology in products, production processes, and administration of small and medium-sized enterprises;
- the strengthening of intercompany cooperation, in the form of networking and industrial environments;
- the development of new products and markets; and
- the enhancement of labor qualifications, especially as regards skills and attitudes towards new technology.

These questions were later formulated in detail, but were included as stated in the description of the evaluation, which was approved later by the steering committee of the NordTek.

The design of the evaluation was also included in its description. It was a multicase study design, the units being six of the major projects under the NordTek. The projects were selected jointly by the evaluation researchers and the program director at the County of North Jutland. The case study design was chosen in agreement. Both sides wanted full data on the program's outcome and causal mechanisms, and the design also gave the managers of the selected projects the opportunity of receiving from the evaluation, information that could be in the management of the projects.

When formulating the evaluation questions (Patton, 1986), the evaluators used an approach focused on utilization, and they also asked the Ministry of Industry and Commerce, as well as the ERDF in Brussels to suggest other aspects for evaluation. However, the ERDF in Brussels did not want to interfere, and the Ministry accepted the original proposal. The formulation of the evaluation questions and the choice of design were made in interaction between the research institute and the program director at the regional level. However, other levels of government stood by in the wings and could have crucially influenced the process, either through the formal forum of the steering committee and board or through informal contacts. But because the negotiation of the evaluation did not give rise to any conflict, the other levels of government acted as a passive audience.

The evaluation was organized, as was usual with AKF research projects. A small project group of researchers was formed and operated with a high degree of autonomy within the evaluation time schedule and budget framework. The evaluation was implemented from September 1988 until June 1991, with data collection to be completed by March 1991.

AKF attached an advisory group to the evaluation team. This group consisted of representatives from national government (Ministries), regional government (the program's administration and planning department at the county of North Jutland), the National Association of Local Authorities, university researchers, and the Business Council of the Labor Movement. That is, two levels of government were directly represented, and one indirectly (the local level). The advisory group met two or three times a year to discuss the progress of the evaluation and the level of consensus was high. Many of the members already knew one another and their approach to the evaluation was constructive. The intermediary evaluation reports were discussed as well as the draft final report. The high degree of consensus in the advisory group and the acceptance of a regional ownership of the program by national and local levels, meant that the interest of other stakeholders in the evaluation was not expressed. Also, the social norm of not interfering with the evaluation tasks of the research institute probably silenced other points of view regarding evaluation design and focus.

The Methods of the Evaluation: Minimizing its
Risk for the Two Operative Levels of Government

In cooperation with the program director, six projects were selected as cases to be evaluated. The selection criteria were that the projects should represent maximum variation in intervention strategies and in localization. They should have received considerable funding from the Program and should all be directed towards companies (not research or administration). The five projects[5] that were eventually evaluated represented such a breadth and share of the whole NordTek Program that the effects achieved through them so far must be deemed to cover important trends in the program as a whole.

Together the selected NordTek projects received 5 million ecus in NordTek grants. The start-up of the various projects was staggered and followed several years preparation, during which ideas were formulated and studies carried out. The evaluation focused on the periods when the project was in operation. By the end of the evaluation, March 1991, the five NordTek projects had been operational for three or more years.

The selection of the six projects as study cases was obviously a strategic choice but given the criteria agreed by the Research Institute as well as the program director, the selection was not problematic. It was openly recognized that the projects with the best chances of success had been selected. The cases represented the "best cases" of the program. Nevertheless, one of the promising projects did not succeed and was shut down because of lack of users in the industry.

The field work of the evaluation was done from autumn 1988 until the end of 1990, ending one year before the program was actually terminated. Initially the evaluation should have ended at same time as the program, but the program was extended by one year. The steering committee of the program wanted to have the evaluation results at that time because they hoped to use the results to obtain development funding from ERDF for future programs in the region.

The data collection was done at two operational levels. At the project level, the evaluators visited each of the projects four or five times over the two-year period. The project managers were interviewed each time, and each project kept records of its activities and users, the record keeping being especially designed for evaluation purposes. These records were analyzed, fed back to the managers and discussed during the visits. The data collected from the enterprises at the other level were also fed back to the project managers. These data were based on visits and interviews with a sample of sixty-eight small and medium-sized enterprises that had been using the services provided by the projects. Finally, in March 1991 forty small and medium-sized enterprises that did not use the services were interviewed by phone.

The data were primarily collected from the projects and from the small and medium-sized enterprises. One should remember that each project was a semi-autonomous unit staffed by 4 to 15 persons, and a board with representation from the municipality and from local business and labour market organizations. These projects were expected to become self-financing and survive after the closure of the NordTek Program. Data in the form of administrative records were also provided from the program department in the county. Basically, however, the prime data for the evaluation were collected in cooperation with the projects and from their users. Data processing and analysis were done in the AKF, the Institute of Local Government Studies, Denmark.

Dissemination of Evaluation Findings: Different Information Needs were not Expressed

The preliminary findings were presented to, and discussed with, each project manager and with the program director. They were also discussed by the evaluation advisory group, which meant that the representatives from the national level (the Ministry of Planning and the Ministry of Industry and Commerce) were included in the discussions too. This kind of ongoing dissemination of the preliminary findings and opportunities for discussing them was a formative element of the evaluation, and was expected to further the subsequent utilization of the evaluation results.

The draft of the final report was also discussed with the advisory group. The concluding chapter was discussed at length, and minor additions were made. The most active members were the representatives from the regional level. For them, the final report would express the degree of success or failure of the program and thus the performance of the program administration. It was a personal matter. The evaluation findings did not involve representatives from the other levels of government personally to any comparable degree. Another reason why the representatives at national and local government level did not have a strong stake in the evaluation conclusion was its content. The conclusion was "soft" in that the time frame of the evaluation made it difficult to determine the longer-term economic effects of the program.

The ongoing dissemination of the evaluation findings took place at three levels of government, most intensively at the local level (the projects) and the regional level (the county). In the advisory group the findings were discussed by representatives from all three levels, the local level being indirectly represented through the National Association of Local Governments. The county played an active part in disseminating the findings by writing a few pages as a postscript to the final report.

After the final report was published August 1991 (all research reports from the Institute of Local Government Studies, AKF, must be accessible to the public), it was sent to key persons at all four levels of government, including the ERDF in Brussels; it was circulated to the relevant Danish organizations and to all the staff of the five programs. The English summary was widely circulated internationally.

The NordTek evaluation was one of the first research-based evaluations of the ERDF program, and was therefore of interest. It was used to argue the need for increased ERDF funding, by presenting documented examples of promising projects from the NordTek Program.

Utilization of the Evaluation Findings: Different Uses at Different Levels

Utilization of research findings is regarded as a process moving forward from the adoption, diffusion, commitment, and institutionalization, in other routines and contexts, of the findings and perspectives of an evaluation (Beyer and Trice 1982). Also different types of utilization have been identified in the literature.

One should expect to find different needs for use at different levels of government. The operational levels of government should be expected to use the findings instrumentally to improve the running of the actual program, but also to use the evaluation findings to legitimize their operations vis-à-vis boards, steering committees and upper levels of government. The levels of government not involved in the actual implementation of the program should be expected to use the evaluation findings in a conceptual way to get ideas to shape future programs, or ideas to evaluate other programs of the same kind or to control lower levels of government.

So how was this evaluation used by various levels of government? There has been no research to answer that question. Therefore, the following statements are based on the author's impressions and experience as well as on contacts with key potential users. They should not be regarded as definitive.

At the project level, the staff used the findings to develop the projects' services and tasks and adjust them to the needs of their clients (the small and medium-sized enterprises). They did that on the basis of feedback from the evaluators. Normally, the staff valued the richness of the evaluation, especially where the small and medium-sized enterprises were concerned, and the exchange of experience and perspectives with the evaluators. In some instances they also used the findings in negotiations with external partners and in marketing. At the project level, the use was mainly instrumental in assisting management, but there was also evidence of conceptual use, that is better understanding of how the small and medium-sized enterprises responded to the services.

In some instances, the evaluation findings were used symbolically as information to the board. The instrumental ongoing use seems the most important. The formative aspect of the evaluation has been a prerequisite for the emergence of "real time" use by management.

At the regional level, the main stakeholders of the evaluation findings were the program staff and the politicians in the county council most closely connected to the program. The results of the NordTek evaluation were discussed at the county level between the program director and the chairmen respectively of the NordTek board and its steering committee. The main user was the program director responsible for program development and implementation. The program staff had an interest in continuous interaction with the evaluators, discussing preliminary findings and perspectives. As such, they were mainly looking for conceptual use of the case study findings, but they also used the findings symbolically. The program administration, the steering committee, and the politicians were responsible for the program, and were thus sensitive as to whether the public regarded it as a success or a failure.

As examples of conceptual use, first the program staff learned from the evaluation to lower their ambitions as to the effect of the program on economic growth in the region. Secondly, the NordTek evaluation made the program director and the board more aware of the need for detailed analyses of the demand side for common infrastructural projects. The NordTek Program had been dominated by a supply orientation, which did not always work sufficiently well. The next generation of regional development programs in North Jutland (RENAVAL and Objective 2) became more oriented towards the demand side.

At the national level, the government's interest in the use of evaluations is dependent upon the role of national government in the ERDF-programs. In Denmark, the ministries' role in these programs has been limited but since they were responsible at national level for co-financing the programs, they should have been more interested in using the evaluation findings for policy purposes. The use of the case-study evaluation has probably been much less at the national level than at the regional and local level, where the main operational responsibility lies. In other countries with other power relationships between regional and central government, the central government's use of evaluation might be more extensive.

At the EU level, there has been at least one instance of conceptual use: the civil servant responsible for ERDF programs in Ireland (and other member states) used an idea from the NordTek evaluation about the survival of the projects after program termination as a criterion for success. The use of a single evaluation from one region in one member state is, however, rare in Brussels (see the following chapter by Jacques Toulemonde). Such evaluations have mainly a symbolic value signalling to the Commission that the region (and the member state) have been in control of the program. The NordTek evaluation was, however, used to press for increased ERDF funding, by presenting documented examples of promising projects from the NordTek Program.

Each level of government has had a number of expected problems and benefits associated with the utilization of the evaluation findings. At the local level the project managers have found that interacting with the evaluator and reading evaluation material are time consuming. On the other hand, having access to rich information about the users' response to the services seems to have made it worthwhile. At the regional level, the problem for the county was the need to act early in order to secure the funding of other programs in the region, and in that respect the evaluation results came too late. However, the authenticity and richness of the case-study evaluation supplemented existing experience. But lack of clear indication of success or failure lowered the symbolic value of the evaluation.

At the national level, government policymakers indicated that they would have appreciated quantitative indicators of the economic effects of the program. The value of the findings lay in the insights into how the program actually operated, and whether or not its potential effects had been achieved. The case-study design also demonstrated how the findings were specific to the region specific, which made extrapolation to other regions uncertain. In Brussels, at the international level, the evaluation demonstrated both the importance of specific national conditions

Figure 5.2
Expected Utilization of NordTek Case Study Evaluations

Level of government	Expected main type of use	Use of case study evaluations, expected problems and benefits
European	Conceptual Symbolic Ex post	– Problems of synthesizing + Knowledge of development process depending upon national context
National	Conceptual Ex post	– Problems of generalization – Need of quantitative indicators of success + Processes contingent upon the nature of the region
Regional	Conceptual On going Ex post	– Problems of timeliness + Authenticity
Local	Instrumental Conceptual Ongoing	– Time-consuming + Richness of information

and the problem of transferability to other member states and to other kinds of ERDF programs. In the EU, the findings from the case studies generated an interest in discovering a way to synthesize these findings with others carried out in the general area of technology transfer. But the problems with synthesizing seem to have been so vast, that the EU has relied instead on single evaluations.

To sum up, the use of the evaluation findings was predominated at the local and regional level, reflecting where the de facto responsibility for program implementation rested. Probably the mere existence of an evaluation demonstrated the willingness of the county to risk an external evaluation, and thus had a symbolic value vis-à-vis the national and EU level, where the use of the evaluation seems to have been modest. The results from the NordTek evaluation can be summarized as follows.

Indirect use of the evaluation findings from the NordTek Program has not been traced, and their use in evaluating programs based on the case study design has not been studied either. However, the evaluator has the impression that the instrumental use has been limited while the conceptual and symbolic use has been more extensive, especially at the levels of government with the main responsibility for program implementation.

As far as the evaluator knows, no joint use of the evaluation ex post across several levels of government has taken place. The use has been within each level of government separately.

Conclusion: Sleeping Partners and the Danish Consensual Tradition

The evaluation of the NordTek Program has been shaped, implemented and used across four levels of government. At different stages of the evaluation process, different levels have been involved and other levels have been "sleeping," that is acting passively towards the evaluation. The different levels of government were interested in different ways in the evaluation and thus had different potential use for the evaluation findings.

This presentation, however, has illustrated that there was no conflict of interest where the evaluation was concerned, and no evidence of conflict regarding the use of the results. What is the explanation of such harmony? Firstly, even when several levels of government were involved at different stages of the evaluation process, the most active was the county at the regional level and the projects at the local level. This reflected the de facto responsibility of the program. The program was implemented quite independently of the national and the European level. There was a high degree of autonomy for the projects at operational level. In that respect, the NordTek was a forerunner of the reform of the EU structural funds that came into effect in 1988 and emphasized regional and local autonomy.

Secondly, to get a more profound understanding of why the intergovernmental evaluation of the NordTek Program was implemented with a high level of consensus by the "sleeping" partners and with modest use of the evaluation at the national and the EU level, one has to take into account the general high degree of autonomy of the Danish local governments (the counties and the municipalities). The two local levels of governments have their economic bases in taxation and their political legitimacy is due to political elections. The local governments supply most of the welfare services, and their share of total public employment is about 60 percent. This tradition of influential and autonomous local governments influences the way other levels of government behave in relation to county-based regional development programs.

Thirdly, this intergovernmental evaluation is related to another cultural aspect of Danish public administration. This aspect has been called the "consensual democracy" and is characterized by a tendency towards avoiding conflicts and willingness to compromise through negotiation. This culture of consensus has been "fertilized" by a long political tradition of minority, multiparty governments and the widespread patterns of cooperation among a huge number of organizations, a kind of societal corporatism (Knudsen, 1992; Elder, Thomas, and Arter, 1983).

In sum, this intergovernmental evaluation seems to have avoided potential tensions among various levels of government by delimiting the focus of evaluation to intermediary program aims, by being conducted in a political setting with a high degree of autonomy at the regional level and within a consensual political culture.

Notes

1. In 1985 the Danish government launched a social experiment with new information technology in local communities. This program resulted from a political compromise about the national computer network. It aimed to compensate for the fact that the network would not reach small rural communities. Sixteen local governments were involved in the social experiments which ran from 1986–1989 with a total local, regional and national financing of DKK 85.5 million (Cronberg et al., 1991).

2. North Jutland fulfilled some special conditions that helped its funding by the ERDF. Politically, a prominent politician in the Social Democratic Party, Poul C. Dalsager, recommended the County of North Jutland to apply for ERDF funding. Mr. Dalsager, a native of North Jutland and a member of government at county level, was a member of the EU Commission from 1981 to 1984. A politician in the Liberal Party (Venstre) and minister in several Danish governments, Henning Christoffersen, was appointed member of the Commission in 1984 and from 1989 onwards had special responsibility for the coordination of the structural funds (including ERDF grants). Politically, therefore, North Jutland had important personal links with the Commission.

   As for access to specialized knowledge, the regional based university, AUC, in the regional capital, Aalborg, was foremost in providing information and staff for the start-up office in the county. One of the civil servants in the county played a crucial role in the preparation of the application to the ERDF when he was employed in the relevant General Directorate (DG 16) in the EU. Consequently, the County of North Jutland has direct personal contacts with key persons in the EC and the ERDF, and could bypass the Danish Ministry of Commerce.

3. The reader should have in mind that the author of this article was responsible for the evaluation. He believes, however, that enough time has elapsed, considering that the evaluation was terminated June 1991 (three years ago) and that neither himself, nor his Research Institute, is dependent on the County of North Jutland in any way.

4. The Institute is funded partly by a basic grant from the County and Municipal Foundation for Education and Research and partly by contributions from local and central governmental agencies, research councils, international organizations and non-profit institutions. In 1992, the total turnover of AKF amounted to DKK 25 million with twenty-five researchers and twenty part-time research assistants.

5. The five projects were: Elektronik Centralen (EC) in Aalborg, a technology service unit belonging to the electronics department; Erhvervs Udviklings Center Farsø (EUC), a business development center for the furniture and wood industry; Hadsund Uddannelses Center (HUC), an educational center; Nordjysk InformatikRåd (NIR), a consultancy unit within informatics; and TEKNORD in Sindal, consultants in technology managing. The technology and product development center for the Mariager Fjord district in Hadsund, which was initially treated as a separate project in the evaluation, was later merged with HUC. EUC closed down and was sold to a furniture manufacturer at the beginning of 1991.

References

Beyer, Janice M. and Harrison M. Trice (1982). "The Utilization process: A Conceptual Framework and Synthesis of Empirical Findings." *Administrative Science Quarterly*, 27 (1982): 591–622

Cronberg, Tarja et al. (eds.) (1991). *Danish Experiments: The Social Construction of Technology*. Copenhagen: New Science Monographer.

Elder, N., A.H. Thomas, and D. Arter (1983). *The Consensual Democracies? The Government and Policies of the Scandinavian States*. Oxford: Martin Robertson.

Heide, H. Ter (ed.) (1990). *Technological Change and Spatial Policy*, Netherlands Geographical Studies 112. Amsterdam, Utrecht: The Hague.

Knudsen, Tim (1992). "A Portrait of Danish State Culture." In M. Kellstrup, ed., *European Integration and Danish Participation*. Copenhagen: Copenhagen Political Studies Press.

Patton, Michael Quinn (1986). *Utilization—Focused Evaluation*. Beverly Hills, CA: Sage Publication.

Rieper, Olaf, Regis Blais, and Anders Larsen (1988). *Information Technology as a Means for Community Development: Telehouses in Scandinavia and Videotex in France*.[PUBLISHER?]

Rieper, Olaf (1991). "Enterprises and Programs for Regional Technological Development." In Tarje Cronberg et al., eds. *Danish Experiments—Social Constructions of Technology*. Copenhagen: The Danish Social Science Research Council, New Social Science Monographs.

Rist, Ray C. (ed.) (1990). *Program Evaluation and the Management of Government*. New Brunswick: Transaction Publishers.

6

Europe and the Member States: Cooperating and Competing on Evaluation Grounds

Jacques Toulemonde

The Sharing of Powers: An Open Debate in Europe

From the Treaty of Rome in 1957 to the Treaty of Maastricht in 1992 the European Union (EU) has, in little more than thirty years, laid the foundations of its sovereignty. What was at first a diplomatic negotiation between independent states has now taken the form of a particular type of government with its own legitimacy, recognized jurisdiction, and autonomous policymaking capacity. However, this construction has been carried out under the watchful eye of the member states who formally decide upon every transfer of power and continue to monitor the growth of European sovereignty, even though it is developing at their expense.

The construction of Europe has often been thought of as an inevitable long-term future event. Now as European policies unfold, their impact is being considered in the present tense, and the question of their limits is very much to the fore. This is one reason for the preeminence of the current debate surrounding subsidiarity.

In 1990, the "Giscard d'Estaing" Report proposed that this principle should be included in the basic treaties in the following terms: "Where powers are not exclusively or completely devolved to the European level, the latter only acts if its intervention is more effective than that of the member states acting separately." Finally, the principle of subsidiarity was integrated into the Treaty of Maastricht in 1992 by the heads of states and governments. The concept in use in Brussels, including the definition above, ignores one historical meaning of the word. Subsidiarity does not only mean preventing a superior level from acting where an inferior level can do better, it also means that the superior level is obliged to act where the inferior level cannot act alone. This second meaning is forgotten more often than not in the current European debate.

With reference to the German origins of the principle, certain sources maintain that it can only be applied if the attributions of each level of government are defined in a clear, constitutional context. Similarly, the 1990 Parliamentary Report proposes to hand over the implementation of the principle to the highest European jurisdiction: the European Court of Justice. However, the Court's former president, Lord Mackenzie Stuart, feels that this is a political issue, unsuitable for judges. Instead of a legal conception that would be necessarily rigid, some would rather see a softer form of subsidiarity, in which no division of powers would be final and in which a process of political arbitration would decide in each case whether an operation was more appropriate, necessary and effective at the European level or national level (Greschmann, 1992).

The frontiers of European policies have been in perpetual movement for the last thirty years and it is unlikely that this movement will be stabilized by any constitutional formula. I therefore think that the soft version of subsidiarity will prevail. Far from freezing responsibilities by means of laws and constitutions, this soft form of subsidiarity relies on political decisions in order to regularly review and reshape policy domains across levels of government. Such political decisions are taken on the basis of effectiveness, and that of one level in relation to another. Such comparison of effectiveness across levels of government could be one reason for systematically undertaking intergovernmental evaluations (IGE). Is this the case in reality?

This chapter will look into European evaluation practice in order to answer the following questions:

- Are there European evaluations which are carried out in an intergovernmental fashion?
- Is there any European evaluation which makes a comparison of effectiveness across levels of government?
- Is intergovernmental evaluation likely to help put the principle of subsidiarity into practice?

European Institutions: Two Levels of Government

It is common to see European institutions presented in a triangular form, with the Parliament, the Council and the Commission, which can be compared to some extent to the American House, Senate, and Executive (Quermonne, 1990). This presentation has some meaning when European political powers are examined from a static viewpoint, but it is totally unsuitable when they are analyzed as part of a dynamic construction process.

The Commission and the Parliament obviously belong to the European level of government. As far as new attributions are concerned, the European Parliament only has an advisory role and will play a very small part in this chapter. The European Commission is certainly the body that represents most effectively a European level of government. It both proposes and executes European policies. It is entrusted with the responsibility of suggesting and designing new regulations and improvements in the fundamental treaties. It also implements all European policies and programs through twenty-three Directorates-General with a total staff of about 15,000. The European Commission (EC) is managed by a collegial board of seventeen commissioners (at the time of writing) appointed for four years by the national governments.

Nevertheless, the Commission's position is rather fragile in the debates surrounding subsidiarity. All the major decisions concerning the construction of the European Union have taken the form of international treaties or unanimous decisions by national governments: Common Market (Rome, 1957), autonomous budgetary resources (1970), European Monetary System and direct universal suffrage (1979), extension of majority voting (Single European Act, 1985), single currency and common foreign policy (Maastricht, 1992). Despite the federalist aims of some of the founding fathers, the Union has been, and continues to be, built by diplomatic negotiations between member states.

The national level continues to represent the main basis of power in the Union, especially as far as extension or limitation of powers is concerned. Member states exercise their powers through the European Council, with semestrial meetings of heads of state and government, and more frequent meetings of ministers. Unanimous voting is used to decide on changes in powers, although more and more current decisions are taken by a majority vote.

The European Council must be regarded as representing the national governments in the European institutions. It is chaired by the member states who each perform six-month periods of office and has practically no staff of its own. These two facts alone make it clear that the Council is not equipped to express interests other than national ones. The Council is relayed by a multitude of administrative committees that examine all European policy decisions in great depth. These committees are made up of national civil servants from the member states. The number and role of these committees are such that the European Union has been referred to as a government of committees (Sidjanski, 1989). The officials of the Commission have even coined a new word for this system of interacting with the national level: "comittology." There exist no less than twenty official administrative committees for the common agricultural policy alone, to which are attached fifty less formal consultative committees. Finally, and according to the definitions in the introductory chapter of this book, the European institutions encompass two levels of government, the European level represented by the Commission (and the Parliament) and the level of the member states acting within the Council.

The Council and the Parliament have few means of their own and so it is the Commission that carries out the real business of evaluation. Evidence of European evaluation practice can be found in a survey dating from 1990 (Sensi and Cracknell, 1991). The survey identified sixteen evaluation units whose total operations involved about fifty persons per year, mostly economists. Having added external consultancy work, the total number of people involved in evaluating European policies amounts to around 150 persons per year. This may seem low compared to American standards, but it must be remembered that the European administration is relatively small. The European budget represents only 1 percent of the national budgets and the whole Commission's staff is smaller than that of a department in a small European country. Moreover, evaluation work has developed rapidly. Out of the sixteen evaluation units surveyed, only two had been in existence for more than five years and the results of the 1990 survey have been rapidly outdated by recent developments.

When questioned about the use to which their work is put, those in charge of the evaluation units mainly consider that their work has internal utility and that it leads to an improvement in the performance of European policies (57 percent) rather than acting as a tool for keeping the Council or Parliament informed, or for accounting to them (21 percent). However, is this managerial view of evaluation not misleading to some extent? Several of the Brussels managers questioned agreed that evaluation has developed rapidly because of pressure from outside the Commission and especially from the Council. It is significant that apart from the Directorate-Generals concerned, the first addressees of the evaluation reports are the Council, the Parliament and the member states.

The European Regional Policy: Bilateral Interactions

In its preamble, the Treaty of Rome undertook to strengthen the unity of the economies of the member states and to ensure harmonious development by reducing regional discrepancies. However, until 1975, no legal or financial means were advanced to promote these objectives. This timorous start can be partly explained by the fact that practically all European countries were establishing their own regional policy at the time. The UK, Italy, France, Germany and even smaller countries like Ireland were developing regional policies with objectives similar to those at the European level.

The European Regional Policy got off the ground slowly but its budget has progressively grown to 5 billion ecus per year (6 billion dollars), and represents more than 10 percent of the European budget. The managing role of the Commission has also become more and more important, going from coordinating to co-financing to co-programming. The Regional Policy is now jointly implemented by European, national and regional levels of government in a partenarial way. This partnership involves collaboration between the Commission and each Member State in the form of bilateral contracts (Community Support Frameworks) and joint monitoring (Monitoring Committees). The European Union has thus chosen the opposite of the German system in which the common task of the Federation and the Länder is organized through multilateral meetings involving all Länder at the same time.

In 1988, when the Council decided upon one of the biggest increases in the Regional Policy's budget, it demanded that evaluation should become systematic. This obligation to evaluate has led to hundreds of intergovernmental evaluations and has sparked off unprecedented evaluation activity all over Europe (Rieper, in this volume; Monnier et al., 1991). At the same time, it has become increasingly difficult to synthesize the dozens of evaluation reports which flood into the Commission's offices.

European regional policy is not immune from the current debates surrounding subsidiarity. In this perspective, the Commission foresees lessening its participation at the inferior programming level (Operational Programs) and devoting itself to the superior level (Community Support Frameworks). This new, simplified procedure should be accompanied by a more significant role for the Commission in matters of evaluation. The Commission hopes to develop bilateral, intergovernmental evaluation as a way of partly keeping the policy under its control although the tide of its increasing powers is receding under the rule of subsidiarity.

Evaluation of Euro-Irish Programs: Safeguarding Consensus

Ireland is the country that benefits most from European Regional Policy in terms of financial transfer per head. European aid to Ireland is co-decided through Community Support Frameworks, the first of which was signed by the Commission and the Irish government in 1989 for a period of five years. This vast program amounts to 6.1 billion ecus (7.3 billion dollars), of which 60 percent come from European tax payers. The CSF is implemented by a Monitoring Committee which includes representatives from both levels of government.

During the first negotiations between the Commission and the Irish government, it was decided that the draft contract should be evaluated. This evaluation was commissioned to the Economic and Social Research Institute (ESRI), an Irish independent organization well listened to by national authorities (Bradley and Fitzgerald, 1992). For reasons of technical expertise, ESRI's researchers were involved from the beginning and took part in the preparation of the terms of reference. After several informal contacts between the two levels of government, the evaluation contract was drawn up by the Irish Department of Finance, accepted by the Commission and endorsed by a Monitoring Committee. The evaluation work was paid for from the European aid attributed to Ireland.

The main question posed to ESRI was the following: what is the likely impact of European aid on the economic development of the country in terms of GNP and employment? In other words, could European aid attain the critical mass which would actually allow Ireland to catch up with European economic standards.

The evaluator's work was extremely technical. They broke down the programs into sectors of intervention: transport, training, research, agriculture, and so on. They made estimates of potential impact for every sector, insisting on the impacts in terms of improved competitiveness for Irish enterprise. They also made an estimation of macro-economic effects using a complex econometric model. ESRI concluded that European aid was likely to boost the Irish GNP growth rate by several points. The evaluation revealed, however, that the aid would not allow Ireland to catch up with the rest of Europe.

The ESRI report was submitted to the Irish government and the Commission. It was discussed by the Monitoring Committee and was the subject of special seminars in Brussels and in Dublin. It is interesting to note that administrative and political circles have made extensive use of the results, both at a national and European level. The conclusions were also used by the Irish government in negotiations for the Treaty of Maastricht, and then again by the Irish press at the time of the referendum for ratification of the Treaty. In Brussels, the Commission used the report to explain the rationale of its Regional Policy. The Commission also referred to ESRI's work to convince the rich countries of the need for an increase in the aid to less developed regions.

If we refer back to the intergovernmental profile proposed in the Introduction, we can see that this evaluation was intergovernmental from almost all points of view. From the informal discussions that preceded the commissioning of the evaluation to the utilization of the results in political and administrative debates, both levels of government were always involved and more often than not worked together. This is a typical example of an intergovernmental evaluation that is formally organized on a bilateral basis. It produced widely utilized conclusions and there is no question of querying the interest it generated. However, as far as subsidiarity is concerned, this bilateral evaluation has not proved to be very productive.

How was the problem of subsidiarity perceived at the time? Firstly, it is obvious that the arrival of such a large amount of European funds could not have taken place without encroachment on Irish sovereignty. In fact, most Irish public investments decisions turned out to be joint decisions between the European and national levels. Whenever Brussels agreed with Irish propositions, which was usually the case, the question of subsidiarity was not a critical issue.

But there has been dissent in certain cases. For example, the Commission constantly promotes the concept of indigenous development, based on local economic potential, strengths and traditions in the assisted areas. After signing the Community Support Framework that agreed upon this objective, on several occasions the Irish government expressed its wish that the European funds should be used to help attract inward investments to Ireland, on the grounds that these operations would be more effective in terms of creating employment.

This is a crucial point for subsidiarity. In fact, the European level must promote employment in Ireland but it must also avoid compromising employment elsewhere in Europe by excessive transfers to Ireland. Is Brussels or Dublin best placed to decide how European aid should be used? Should the decision be left to the national level, in the knowledge that the employment criteria will be predominant? Or should the Commission have the last word, given that it has to judge with reference to a wider range of criteria?

There is no question, at this point, of evaluating the complex arguments of this debate. Suffice to note that these arguments were not included in ESRI's evaluation. However, the technique used by evaluators could have allowed useful information to be brought into the debate.[1] This intergovernmental evaluation avoided a sensitive question through a kind of self-censorship, the reason being linked, no doubt, to the process of bilateral evaluation itself.

The evaluation was closely controlled by those implementing the policy at both levels of government. The success of their joint policy and its continuation depended on the consensus they managed to attain within the Monitoring Committee and during subsequent negotiations. It was therefore in their interest not to undermine this consensus by raising controversial questions. Questioning the limits of their responsibilities, for example, was out of bounds, especially as such a question could only be answered in a multilateral debate.

This example clearly shows one of the limitations of bilateral evaluation in the European context. Since the transfer of responsibilities is debated multilaterally, any evaluation of subsidiarity must be multilaterally credible. In spite of its qualities, the evaluation of the Irish CSF remained open to questioning, in that it involved no Member State other than Ireland.

Evaluation of the European R&D Policy: Competing Evaluations

In the 1970s, European programs in the field of Research and Development gradually appeared. When there were enough of them, the Commission proposed giving them a more coherent form. This was how the first, "European Framework Program for R&D," covering the period from 1984–1987, came about. The budget for R&D policy was such that the Single European Act Treaty (1986–1987) ratified its existence and clarified its objective: "To reinforce the scientific and technological basis of European industry and to encourage it to become more competitive internationally." A second and a third program were decided upon by the Council, the third program amounting to 5.7 billion ecus (6.8 billion dollars) and covering the period from 1990–1994.

In spite of its growing importance and its recent recognition, Research and Development Policy remains fragile. Firstly, its budget represents only four percent of public expenditure on research in Europe. This underlines how much more important the national level is compared to the European level in this area, all the more so as each member state has powerful and long-established institutions and policies. Through their representatives in the Council, the member states are well placed to control the extension of Brussels' responsibilities. It is noteworthy that the Framework Program for R&D is still adopted by a unanimous vote in the Council. The Council extends its control over Research and Development Policy through a series of administrative committees made up of national civil servants. The chief committee is the Committee for Scientific and Technical Research, and we will see that this body plays a role in intergovernmental evaluation.

The second European Framework Program included about thirty individual programs ranging from information technology to biotechnology. When the third Framework Program was being voted, the Council asked the Commission to evaluate the work which had been carried out up to that period. The Commission, which formerly had undertaken systematic evaluations of its individual programs, managed to produce a synthesis of its previous findings. During a European Council meeting in April 1992, the national ministers in charge of research congratulated themselves on this work.

However, they considered it insufficient and organized a more in-depth evaluation. This procedure is a new one. It could be said that this was the first time the Council proceeded to carry out an evaluation that was controlled principally by its own services, even though it has practically no staff of its own. This initiative was taken under pressure from Dutch and English representatives who held the presidency during this period.

The Committee for Scientific and Technical Research was entrusted with the organization of the evaluation. With the help of a British academic research center, a questionnaire survey was carried out among the national members of the numerous advisory committees which had been set up for the different programs. This "counter-evaluation" relied heavily, therefore, on the system of committees which represent national interests in the European organization.

The conclusions reached by the "counter-evaluation" did not significantly differ from those of the Commission. Was this perhaps due to a lack of time, means and experience? In fact the national experts who were consulted in the survey had practically no sources of information at their disposal other than the Commission's reports (Toulemonde, 1994). As could be expected, this counter-evaluation dealt with the question of subsidiarity. However, it did not manage to define clear criteria to judge the relative effectiveness of government levels in the management of Research and Development Policy. Finally, the evaluation report limited itself to merely wishing that: "subsidiarity should be part of the essential criteria in the future evaluations of the Commission."

In this particular case the Council attempted to set up a multilateral evaluation capacity, parallel to that of the Commission, in order to create a more balanced debate on the implementation of subsidiarity. It is obvious, however, that the Council has few means at its disposal, and that it cannot back any operation on a long-term basis unless the circumstances are favorable, such as two successive presidencies working in the same direction. The following example demonstrates another path that could be followed so as to strengthen multilateral intergovernmental evaluation of subsidiarity.

Impact of European R&D Programs in France: Informal "IGE"

When the Commission was given responsibility for the co-ordination of National Research and Development Policies in 1974, it set up a unit to observe national policies and pinpoint their developments. In 1985, a series of studies were launched to find out if national strategies had been modified by European policy, and if so, in which direction. About ten of these studies have been carried out and the French one can be used to illustrate the point in question.

In 1989 the Commission ordered an evaluation of "the impact of European programs on the French scientific and technical environment."

The date of the order was chosen so that the results would be available when France took over the presidency of the Council. The evaluation was entrusted to the leading French academic research center in the field of research evaluation (Laredo and Callon, 1990). The evaluators began by making a survey through semistructured interviews with about eighty influential people from the French research milieu. Of these, about ten were chosen to form a steering committee. A questionnaire was then mailed to some 1600 researchers who had received European funding. The results of this survey were submitted to the steering committee for comment.

The evaluation concluded that the European programs, despite bearing little financial weight, had provoked (or encouraged) a significant reorientation of national practices in favor of basic technological research. Subsidiarity was dealt with indirectly by the evaluators through a series of questions about complementarity or duplication between national and European programs. However the report did not reach a clear conclusion on this point and recommended that future evaluations should reinforce this aspect of the work.

This French case presents several characteristic features. The commissioning and terms of reference came from the European level, but experts from a national level were asked to join a panel to monitor and advise the evaluator. The evaluator himself was chosen for its being credible with national authorities. He submitted his report to the Commission at the time when his country held the presidency of the Council. Thus, every precaution was taken so that the evaluation would be heeded and well received by the national authorities. However, the latter were never officially involved in any stage of the process.

This type of evaluation is an attempt at an interesting compromise between the different contradictions that have been observed in the above examples. It is not formally intergovernmental and as a result, can probably avoid the phenomenon of self-censorship observed in the case of the Irish Community Support Framework. However, it involves both levels of government to a degree sufficient to make it credible for each of them. It is mainly bilateral and this probably limits its capacity to forward the debate on subsidiarity. But it also takes a multilateral form in that it is addressed to a very significant member state: the one that chairs the European Council. It can be assumed that through this type of compromise, intergovernmental evaluation will be able to contribute useful elements to the debate on subsidiarity.

Intergovernmental Evaluation in Europe: Main Conclusions

This study cannot end with clear-cut conclusions since European practice is relatively young, and, above all, it has not become stabilized. However the cases which have been studied are sufficiently varied to enable us to draw certain conclusions which could provide a solid base for further reflection in this field.

IGE Requires a Balanced Evaluation Capacity

It is always possible to improve the quality of the evaluations and it would be appealing to imagine an objective means of measuring the comparative effectiveness of the different levels of government. However, our examples clearly show that it would be utopian to imagine that intergovernmental evaluation can resolve a subsidiarity problem in a purely instrumental manner. The first nontechnical factor to be taken into account is obviously the balance of powers between the levels of government. In the case of Research and Development Policy, the European level is newer and less legitimate than the national level. The Council (national level) has not hesitated to carry out its own counter-evaluations. This confirms an obviously natural principle: the more legitimate a level of government, the more decisive a role it plays in intergovernmental evaluation.

But expertise in evaluation is also an important resource. In the case of Research and Development, the seniority and experience of the Commission's officials (European level) gave them an unquestionable part to play in the intergovernmental evaluation game, despite the weak legitimacy of the European policy they had to manage. We have already seen that the counter-evaluation organized by the Council did not produce a different judgment, due to the lack of sufficient counter-expertise. An imbalance in terms of legitimacy can thus be compensated by a higher evaluation capacity.

A level of government that has no long-term legitimacy can prove its relevance and demonstrate its effectiveness through a purpose-built evaluation capacity. However, this process is quite time consuming. It has taken the Commission more than a decade, which is probably a reasonable length of time considering the pace of the subsidiarity debate.

Figure 6.1
Characteristics of Three Intergovernmental Evaluations

Evaluation Studied	Intergovernmental Features		
	Formal comprehensive interaction	Common judgment	Information on key questions
Euro-Irish regional programs	yes	yes	no
R&D framework program	yes	no	no
Impact of R&D programs in France	no	no	yes

IGE Works Better When Interaction is Informal

The paragon of intergovernmental evaluation would be a procedure in which several levels of government formally take part and produce a common judgment, based on the most comprehensive information. Formal interaction means that government is present in the evaluation process in the form of representatives who play an official role on behalf of their institution. On the contrary, informal participation could involve an evaluation steering committee which stakeholders of different levels attend on a personal basis. An evaluation can be considered comprehensive if it informs on sensitive key questions. On the other hand, an evaluation only partially informs if data on critical judgment criteria are ignored.

None of the cases studied meet all three of the criteria of the ideal IGE as listed in figure 6.1. In the case of the impact of European R&D programs in France, the national level was not officially involved in the evaluation process. In the case of the Science and Technology Framework Program, two levels of government are formally involved: European with the Commission, and national with the Council. However, there was no intention of coming up with a common judgment, even though the conclusions of the two parallel evaluations only differ very slightly. The case of the Irish Community Support Framework is the closest to an ideal definition. Both levels of government were formally represented and the evaluation aimed at producing a common judgment. However we have already observed that an important criterion of judgment was omitted to avoid compromising the joint-management of the policy. The information provided by this evaluation was therefore not as comprehensive as it could have been. In any event, the analysis of these cases demonstrates that it is extremely difficult for a single evaluation to combine all three key intergovernmental features. When several levels of government *formally* take part in an evaluation procedure, the competing demands and needs become structural antagonisms.

IGE Requires a Mix of Bilateral and Multilateral Processes

The principle of subsidiarity prevents a higher level from acting where a lower level can do better. The European situation is special in that the lower level includes large, powerful countries like Germany or United Kingdom and smaller ones like Belgium or Ireland. Some policies, merger control for example, can be efficiently implemented in large member states while being less successful in smaller ones. It appears that subsidiarity should apply differently, depending on the size of the authorities at the lower level. This seems to imply a case-by-case study of the effectiveness of the governments involved.

The problem is clear-cut when it comes to regional policy. The sphere of effectiveness of the European level is obviously greater in the case of Ireland, which faces severe development problems, than in the Netherlands, which is at the forefront of the European economy. Does this prove that the evaluation of subsidiarity must be bilateral? A study of European practice provides a rather qualified answer.

The evaluations that have been studied reveal the following: in all cases the conclusions legitimized the European areas of responsibilities, even if they criticized the Commission on details. This can be explained by the fact that the Commission controlled the process in its totality or for the most part (the impact of R&D in France), or that conflicting questions were left aside (the case of the Irish CSF), or that the counter-expertise at national level was insufficient (the case of the Research and Development Framework Program). It can therefore be assumed that, in general, the national level does not play a significant part in European evaluations[2].

Member states would obviously carry more weight if intergovernmental evaluations were organized on multilateral lines[3]. If this were the case, national governments could compensate for their relative weakness by speaking with a single "multilateral" voice. In the European context, multilateral involvement of member states would necessarily go through the Council and via the committees system. If intergovernmental evaluation is to become more multilateral for reasons of political weight, it must also remain bilateral for sensible reasons which have been set out above, each Member State having its own specificity. Thus, a balance has yet to be achieved between bilateral and multilateral evaluation.

Balancing Contradictory Criteria

The case of the Irish CSF demonstrates that evaluation criteria are not necessarily the same at each level of government. The national level favors the criterion of job creation whereas the Commission favors indigenous development and job creation.

Comparing the effectiveness of several levels of government goes far beyond a problem of measurement because the measuring standards (criteria of judgment) differ from one level to the next. It could almost be said that the evaluation of subsidiarity should not look for the most effective level of government, as the common definition would suggest, but for the level of government that ensures the best choice between contradictory criteria of effectiveness.

Conclusion

Evaluations only become truly intergovernmental when powers are sufficiently balanced. Such a balance does not depend merely on institutional strengths and budgetary weights. A level of government which is not in a favorable position can compensate its weakness by excellent evaluation capacities. If the less favored governments are at the lower level, they can also compensate for their weakness by speaking with a single "multilateral" voice. Evaluations which go further in addressing intergovernmental questions are also those which are less formally implemented and which clearly stem from diplomacy. As long as officials formally participate in an evaluation on behalf of their institutions, they do not allow their respective effectiveness to be judged in a comparative fashion.

These are the main conclusions which can be drawn from a study of present European practice. They will probably apply in the future if intergovernmental evaluation is to fuel the permanent process of reshaping the European institutional landscape.

Notes

1. The Hermes econometric model, which was used by ESRI, distinguishes between two industrial sectors: national industry and multinational firms.
2. It is interesting to note that the French government recently carried out an important intergovernmental evaluation of subsidiarity in an informal and multilateral context. This evaluation concerned the process of "Planning Contracts" between the national state and the regions. These contracts are signed for five years between the state and each of the twenty-two French regions. They are similar to the European CSF, for which they were used, in part, as a model. The evaluation was ordered by the prime minister and carried out in 1992 by the national administration (unpublished report). Several representatives from the regional level were invited to take part personally in the evaluation work, from the formulating of the questions to the discussion of the final report. The evaluation dealt with several sensitive problems relating to subsidiarity.
3. This recommendation resembles the German practice of multilateral joint-management of regional policy in the context of the common task (*Gemeinschaftsaufsgabe*) between the Federal government and the *"Länder."* This practice has given rise to intense activity in intergovernmental evaluation, especially in the assessing of eligibility criteria for assisted areas.

References

Bradley, J.and J. Fitzgerald (1992). "The Role of the Structural Funds: Analysis of Consequences for Ireland in the Context of 1992." *Policy Research Series,* 13. Dublin: Economic and Social Research Institute.

Greschmann, K. (1992). "Le principe de subsidiarité: quelles responsabilités à quel niveau de pouvoir dans une Europe intégrée?" In EIPA (ed.) *Subsidiarité, défi au changement.* Maastricht: EIPA.

Laredo, Ph. and M. Callon (1990). *L'impact des programmes communautaires sur le tissu scientifique et technique français.* Paris: Centre de Sociologie de l'Innovation.

Monnier, E. et al. (1991). *Programme européen d'analyse méthodologique pour l'évaluation des politiques structurelles: étude de définition.* Lyon: ENTPE-CEOPS.

Quermonne, J.L. (1990). "Existe-t-il un modèle politique européen?" *Revue Française de Sciences Politiques,* 40/2, 208.

Rieper, O. (1994). "Evaluation of an EU-Funded Regional Development Program in Denmark," this volume.

Sensi, D. and B. Cracknell (1991). *Inquiry into Evaluation Practices in the Commission.* Luxembourg: Office des publications de la Commission Européenne.

Sidjanski, D. (1989). "La Communauté Européenne: un gouvernement de comités?" *Pouvoirs,* 48.

Toulemonde, J. (1995). "Peut-on évaluer la subsidiarité? Eléments de réponse inspirés de la pratique européenne," forthcoming.

7

Evaluation of the Federal Office of Environmental Protection: Across Two Levels of Government

Willi Zimmermann and Peter Knoepfel

In the beginning was a conflict between the Swiss parliament and a federal ministry. In the end, an institution, a federal agency was evaluated. At the very beginning, the question was whether the merging of two federal agencies would mean the creation of a higher organizational unit, for which parliamentary approval would have been necessary, or whether it was simply a question of merging the two agencies to form the Federal Office for Environmental Protection (FOEP). In the end, this new federal agency was the subject of an evaluative study which is discussed here.

Point of Departure: Policy Orientation Replaces the Business Management Approach

The authors of this essay were appointed by the Federal Parliament Auditing Commission to analyze the implementation of environmental policy in Switzerland and clarify the following specific issues:

- the ability of the FOEP structure to guarantee the homogeneity and effectiveness of environmental policy;
- the execution of environmental conservation measures from the point of view of the organization of the federal agency. FOEP structures were to be analyzed in the light of this execution; and
- the difficulties facing cantonal authorities in the execution of environmental policy measures.

The Parliamentary Auditing Commission decided to abandon the business-management approach because one of the two agencies and their merger had previously been evaluated using such an approach. It opted instead for a policy-oriented approach because this involved the evaluation of internal and external organizational structures in the light of their administrative output, and the evaluation of the relations between the two agencies. This interaction takes place at both federal and cantonal level; our IGE is of the managerial type (as defined in the Introduction).

The evaluators, therefore, worked on the assumption that there is an inherent link between an administrative product and the administrative structures and processes involved in its production. In the case of the FOEP, the hypothesis was that the production of a consistent, coherent administrative product necessitates organizational structures and decision-making processes with a specific capacity for coordination. It is important to note here that policy-oriented administrative analyses are based on a policy concept which is not restricted to parliamentary or government decisions. The concept of "public policy" as used in the Anglo-Saxon context (the French use *politique publique* and the Italians, *politica pubblica*) is actually more accurate here as this concept covers the sum of public decisions and measures used in the solution of collective problems. These may be legislative, administrative, legal, and sometimes even social or associative in nature and can occur at the federal, cantonal, and even local authority level.

The entire contribution of a particular authority or administrative body to such a public policy is known as its policy in the area in question (according to the traditional designation: "practical" or "management"). Thus, for example, in the area of clean air, it is possible to distinguish between a FOEP policy, a policy of canton XY or a policy of the federal government or parliament. This policy concept is purely analytical in nature; it has nothing to say about the contradictory relationship, for example, between a federal agency policy and that of the relevant federal minister or the federal government. This does not broach the (always controversial) issue of the extent to which a federal agency has the right to make "political" decisions, or the extent to which it actually makes such decisions of political value independent of legal competence. In this study, "FOEP policy" is understood as the sum of measures and decisions implemented and taken by this agency in the solution of specific environmental problems on the basis of existing legal provisions.

In accordance with the task set by the Federal Parliament auditing commission, the aim of this study was to evaluate the quality of the FOEP's entire administrative output in different environmental areas between 1985 and 1991 from the point of view of the experience of the cantons, and the reactions of other important federal agencies. A secondary aim involved the identification of the organizational or procedural causes of possible errors within the FOEP. The main focus in the evaluation of the FOEP's activities was on clean air policy. In addition to this policy field, which is linked in many ways to other areas of environmental policy, activities connected with environmental impact assessment were also studied, and finally, water conservation for agricultural purposes was also examined. It should be noted that other important FOEP activities such as soil conservation and waste management were not included in the evaluation.

The evaluation was, therefore, undertaken from the perspective of the effective implementation of the legal aims of environmental policy. Other policies that, on the basis of their specific tasks or specific interpretations by their ministries and federal agencies involve aims that tend to contradict those of environmental policy, are seen as potentially restrictive factors. The analysis of effectiveness focuses on services provided by the various offices of the federal agencies which are directly involved in environmental policy, and the FOEP in particular. Together, these offices constitute an open sociopolitical system. Such systems are characterized firstly by the way in which they accept and adequately deal with impulses from their environment (other agencies, cantons, international contexts), and the way in which they inform their environment of their aims, so that these can be observed.

Few economic studies have hitherto been undertaken on administrative bodies in Switzerland. Those that are available do not provide any clear guidelines on the methods which should be used. For this reason we have based our approach in part on our research experience and in part on new methodological elements.

Execution of the Evaluation

To ensure optimum accuracy and comprehensiveness, we used a specific combination of quantitative surveying (questionnaires) and qualitative information (analysis of documentation and interviews). Moreover, we took a bottom-up approach in the interviews that involved first interviewing those staff members in subordinate positions within the hierarchy of the agencies in question. The interviews provided an opportunity to consider in greater depth the questionnaires answered by these people and to discuss their experiences relating to environment policy, using examples from actual cases. The most important results of these intensive interviews were presented for verification/opinion to the employees at the next level in the hierarchy (so-called cross-interviews). The latter also questioned about their own questionnaires and on subjects of relevance to their work and experience.

The first step in the evaluation involved the implementation of a quantitative survey in the twenty-six cantons and used a questionnaire for this purpose. The relevant cantonal ministers were asked to fill out a questionnaire themselves and distribute questionnaires among colleagues responsible for environmental conservation (usually the environmental conservation offices). Of the 130 questionnaires dispatched, eighty-nine were returned. At 68 percent, this response is deemed satisfactory.

A total of sixteen cantonal ministers and all twenty-six directors of the cantonal environmental conservation offices participated in the quantitative survey. In-depth discussions about the results of this survey were held with officials from four cantons. One of the additional aims of the evaluation was to assess the nature of concrete cooperation between the FOEP and the specialized cantonal bodies. Prior to the discussions, we reconstructed this cooperation with the help of documents. Three relevant cases were prepared for each canton. These cases involved: (1) the redevelopment of a waste water unit and water conservation for agricultural purposes; (2) environmental impact assessment; (3) the production of the cantonal plan for clean air policy. The FOEP was and is strongly involved in all of these cases. We evaluated the nature of the cooperation between the cantonal and federal agencies on the basis of this dossier and presented our framework to the cantonal officials for their views.

The methodological approach used for the cantonal organizations was also used for FOEP itself. A comprehensive questionnaire on the main subject was distributed to all persons (318) working in the agency. The questions dealt with the organizational and management structure of the agency, the capacity for innovation in the agency, communication inside and outside the agency, specialized knowledge and perception of problems. The three cases listed above were also mentioned and those employees involved in clean air policy, waste water disposal, water conservation for agricultural purposes and environmental impact assessment were asked special questions. Of the questionnaires 248 (78 percent) were suitable for statistical assessment. The qualitative survey was then implemented on the basis of these results. This involved one and a half-hour conversations with a total of forty-four employees of the FOEP.

The Auditing Commission also requested that important federal agencies be included in the evaluation and questioned about their experience in cooperation with the FOEP. We selected those agencies defined as "difficult" partners in the written questionnaire completed by the FOEP employees. The agencies in question were those whose policy areas can be described, among other things, as extremely "harmful to the environment" and include: the police, public transport, Federal Agriculture Office, highway construction and external commercial relations. These interviews lasted sixty to 150 minutes and were normally conducted with at least two persons. At the end of this evaluation phase, discussions were also held with the minister and general secretary of the Ministry of the Interior responsible for environmental protection. The following points were discussed at these talks: the results of both questionnaires, the vertical and horizontal cooperation within and outside the FOEP, the quality of standard material, models and vision, informal structures, the FOEP corporate identity and proposals for reorganization.

Difficulties Encountered in the Implementation of Scientific Evaluation in Federal Contexts

Before going into some of the difficulties encountered in the implementation of this evaluation, it is necessary to give a short description of the Swiss political system.

Switzerland is a country with many special features. Its political system does not neatly fit any of the current theories of the modern state. Some of the most important elements of the political system are the following: (1) new problems are, if possible, solved by private means, the state takes second place; (2) if political action is required, the closest possible cooperation is sought in many political fields. Social partnership is well established; and (3) The system includes institutions such as referendums and popular initiatives[1].

Another distinctive feature of Swiss political organization is the federal system. This consists of three political levels: (1) the Confederation with the Swiss government, the Federal Administration which has its own budget and the Federal Assembly or Parliament with its two chambers, the National Council which represents the Swiss people and the Council of States which represents the cantons[2]; (2) The twenty-six cantons, each with its own cantonal government, parliament, administration and budget; and (3) the 3,029 local (political) communes with their own governments, modes of representation, administration and budget[3], which, however, always act within the scope of their respective cantonal context.

Federalism is achieved in a number of ways. According to the Swiss Constitution, the twenty cantons and six half-cantons are members of the federal state. They are not sovereign states as they were in the past; however, they are distinct political entities with their own traditions. Each canton has its own constitution and a set of laws to regulate its internal affairs. The cantons have considerable scope for participation in the formulation of legislation and decision making at the federal level through their participation in the Council of States, the federal referenda and the preparliamentary consultation procedure[4]. The cantons also play a decisive role in many political domains when it comes to the execution of federal legislation. For this reason, the system is often referred to as one of "*Vollzugsfederalismus*" (executive federalism). As a general rule, it is possible to say that the Confederation defines the aims of a public policy while the cantons choose the means of implementation and execute it in the form of individual projects. This structure should be kept in mind when reading the following paragraphs.

Difficulties were encountered in the execution of the evaluation. As a first step, a quantitative survey was undertaken in the cantons. The questionnaires were sent to the competent cantonal ministers who were asked to pass them on to the officials responsible for environmental issues within the canton administration. For political reasons, it would have been inconceivable for experts appointed by the Parliamentary Auditing Commission to approach the cantonal offices directly without first approaching the cantonal governments. This meant that, inevitably, the experts did not have complete control over the entire survey. All of the cantons responded, though one canton only returned one questionnaire. The willingness of the cantons to participate in the evaluation can generally be described as positive.

Another difficulty arose from the fact that it was almost impossible to discuss the organizational problems in isolation from the general structural, management and personnel problems within the entire FOEP and its political environment. The administrative-scientific analysis of the FOEP output and its identification with key individual departments within the FOEP was not very productive for several reasons. Firstly, the legal analysis revealed few contradictions between the different environmental decrees. Thus, this analysis of origins proved to be not absolutely necessary. Also, the output was shown to have a predominantly natural science and engineering content[5].

A third problem lay in the fact that the responsibility for the processing of a document could usually be traced to a specific department; however, within the internal development of objectives within the agency, it was difficult to reconstruct the number of actors involved in retrospect. Other departments, the administration, the general secretariat and the department (Ministry of the Interior) were involved in different capacities in the subsequent consultation. Thus, the concrete contributions and influences of all of these actors largely elude empirical documentation. There is no objective measure for the evaluation of statements concerning the FOEP's specific policy and executive services. Our own experience and our (certainly limited) knowledge of the history and development of the relevant policy area was used as a basis for the evaluation. This was combined with the insight gradually gained from the repeated questioning in the discussions with our interviewees from the cantons, FOEP and the representatives from other federal agencies in the course of the survey.

Some Results

We have seen that the federal system consists of several politically autonomous units. These include the federation and the cantons. In general, the cantonal actors gave the FOEP quite good grades. For example, according to these cantonal officials, the FOEP clean air department dealt successfully with the varied aspects and complexity of the problem. The cantonal officials made considerable use of the recommendations, statements, and reports provided by the FOEP. It is worth noting that only a small minority (4 to 6 percent of cantonal answers) were of the opinion that the FOEP's technical language and its political principles were contradictory. The quality of the—extremely frequent—contact with representatives of the FOEP clean air department was described as good to very good. A third of those questioned had absolutely no problems with respect to cooperation with the FOEP, 64 percent admitted to having "some" problems. The problems mentioned had to do with "conflicts of interest between the federation and the canton," "internal problems of coordination within the FOEP," and "lack of availability of FOEP officials."

The cantonal actors, thus, gave the FOEP a rather positive evaluation. They were less positive, however, in their evaluation of the Confederation. The latter includes the federal government and parliament. The questions we asked about the activities of these bodies related to their definitions of legal concepts and norms, their fixing of deadlines, their statements in relation to specific decisions (words versus deeds) and, last but not least, the way in which they made allowance for too many or too few exceptions.

From the point of view of cantonal environmental officials, the Confederate bodies behave in a far more contradictory fashion than the FOEP. This discrepancy can mainly be explained by the functional specialization and professionalization which pervades all three levels of the federal system (federation, canton, bigger towns).This cartelization has the advantage of facilitating the relatively simple and rapid establishment of consensus. This is simple and rapid because the actors involved usually share the same interests and perception of problems, and define reality in the same way. With few exceptions, the cantonal actors attested the goodwill and excellent specialist knowledge of their FOEP colleagues.

However, certain disadvantages within this professionalized sector should not be overlooked. Because they are specialists and are obliged to sell their specialized product to other sectors, the capacity of these actors for action is basically limited. Moreover, increasing specialization heightens the potential for conflict and the frustration of the frontline officials. This is due to the highly technical emphasis in the FOEP's environmental conservation policy, which takes an outlet-of-pipe direction. It is also due to the increasing difficulties associated with policy execution; we assume that these result mostly from the individualization of society and are not directly connected with FOEP's activities. The detailed discussions on the results of the survey (questionnaire) and on the individual cases reviewed with the officials from four cantons revealed that, from their point of view, the technical approach to environmental conservation, and particularly its control, have reached its limits. For this reason it is imperative that it now be complemented with economic measures.

By drawing on the information we obtained from the civil servants, several social developments indicating a trend towards individualization in highly developed West European states were observed: higher levels of income and increased leisure are giving rise to greater individual liberty; economic growth is leading to large-scale (upward) mobility and to the diversification of lifestyles; improved educational opportunities mean greater freedom for the individual to pursue his or her chosen career and greater scope for general personal development. Under such circumstances, public policies lose their steering capacities, it becomes more difficult to implement public laws and protect the environment. The technical outlet-of-pipe solution no longer suffices, for, to put it bluntly, it allows pollution to occur and expects the public authorities to clean up the mess. Pollution must, therefore, be prevented by ways and means that reach out to all members of society, including its unwilling individualists. These ways and means are mainly economic (internalize the cost of pollution). This, at least, was the opinion of most of the civil servants we interviewed. Thus, a clear need for a change in strategy was identified in the area of economic steering and also in the case of the clean air policy.

A positive observation was that the clean air concept, set out in a target-oriented strategic paper, also provided the federal clean air policy with a razor-sharp gauge that was very useful to the cantons in the production of their cantonal plans for a clean air policy and remains so. In addition, the corresponding decree with its unambiguous limit values and the mechanisms for achieving them provides a totally suitable executive instrument. In contrast to the noise pollution decree, the clean air decree only contains a few exceptions that are very clearly formulated. The most significant point about which lack of clarity prevails is the, politically speaking, highly sensitive question of what should be done with new installations in critical polluted areas.

The potential for conflict can, therefore, only be reduced by a change in strategy. The cantonal peers of the FOEP are not the only source of potential conflict; the Office itself is also involved in relatively substantial conflict with numerous federal actors. As an example, we have chosen traffic-related environmental policy. This area is a particularly clear example of the difficult situations which the FOEP must master. In principle, much depends on the decisions taken by other agencies and ministries and the conditions surrounding other policy areas. A typical example is the Federal Police Office which is responsible for signposting and the testing of vehicles. The work of the FOEP, which must guarantee implementation, was not made easier when, for example, officials of several cantons declared in 1991 that in view of the difference in the strict limit values stipulated in the clean air ordinance as compared with those in other countries, it would be advisable for the federal government to reexamine these limit values.

This relativization of environmental conservation policy by polluting actors is not restricted to the clean air policy but can also be found in water conservation for agricultural purposes. It should be noted that FOEP activities in this context received a far less positive evaluation. So far as we can establish from the discussions that were limited to environmental conservation, implementation problems have arisen everywhere as regards the conservation of rural water for agricultural purposes. In contrast to the clean air policy, the FOEP is not seen as helping to speed up cantonal execution. In general, from the perspective of the cantons, the implementation of water conservation for agricultural purposes is disregarded, mainly because the agricultural sector and agricultural authorities in the cantons themselves have problems in this connection. The cantons surveyed made very clear, however, that the regulations and executive aids in the form of recommendations and guidelines etc. provided by the FOEP are not very helpful. For the vast majority of the cantonal officials consulted, the federal government and parliament have not made adequate provision to ensure that water conservation for agricultural purposes is at one with agricultural policy itself. The cantons feel that the Confederation is speaking two different languages in this instance—that of the FOEP and that of the Federal Office of Agriculture.

We have thus established that numerous problems exist within a "transverse" environmental policy that can be traced back in particular to the professionalized sectors. Hence the strong criticism by the administration at the cantonal and federal levels. The two blocs stand face to face. On the one side there are the federal and cantonal "environmental protectors" and on the other the federal and cantonal "environmental polluters" which include the farmers, the police, and the highway construction bodies. The accusations leveled by these bodies at the "environmental protectors" include:

- their interpretation of the legislative basis is narrow and small-minded;
- they do not show any understanding of other policy areas, beyond environmental conservation and the situation of the relevant actors;
- they do not provide comprehensive information and fail to issue invitations to important meetings;
- they deliberately put representatives of other policy areas under pressure to act by setting very tight deadlines; and
- ultimately, the environmental protectors are not interested in the general well-being but pursue only pure and simple environmental policy.

The reproaches leveled by the "environmental protectors" at the "environmental polluters" are the reverse of those listed above.

Looking briefly at the environmental impact assessment policy, we find that none of the cantonal interviewees wanted to dispense fully with the FOEP's participation in this policy (hearing procedure). The federal ordinance on environmental impact assessment lists a certain number of installations which the FOEP must include in the assessment procedure. The interviewees looked on this procedure, together with federal participation, as guaranteeing consistency of approach in the cantons. We noted that, in contrast to the general opinion expressed throughout the country and by numerous cantonal governments in particular, the relevant specialist offices in the cantons along with a clear majority of the authorities consulted, welcome environmental impact assessment as a suitable instrument for the coordinated implementation of federal and cantonal environmental policy. On the basis of information from another study of the Canton of Berne and statements made by cantonal infrastructure departments, we know that this opinion is not unopposed at the level of cantonal administration. The highway construction offices, hydraulic engineering and energy authorities in many areas are of the opinion that environmental impact assessment is an instrument which obstructs construction. They see it as unnecessary, since prior to its existence, the relevant installations were always tested for environmental effects.

The problems with environmental impact assessment have highlighted many instances of a lack of coordination at the program level between different planning policies, particularly environmental conservation in regional planning, forestry, highway construction and waste disposal and dumping. There is a need for material coordination which must be carefully established prior to the allocation of a permit at project level. This gives rise to real delays. There can be no doubt that an environmental impact assessment cannot be blamed for applying an "emergency brake" on this coordination function; rather, the above-mentioned policies and their extremely complex procedural regulations are to blame. Environmental impact assessment is an essential policy instrument for establishing agreement between the various planning policies necessary for the integral implementation of environmental policy.

Some Lessons Learned

Who should perform the evaluation in such cases? Insiders or newcomers? In the present case, the parliamentary commission opted for the former. Why? Prior to being appointed by the commission, the evaluators had already studied and evaluated the implementation of federal legislation in Switzerland—in most instances in relation to environmental conservation. They belong to a rare breed of researchers who have traced the development of a topic (environmental conservation in the agricultural sector) from federal through cantonal and local authority levels to individual farmers.

Why did the commission decide to opt for these insiders? The Federal Auditing Commission is under considerable pressure. Our federal parliament is not a professional body (its sessions last only nine to twelve weeks per year); time is a scarce resource and complex evaluations are time consuming. Secondly, this evaluation provided an opportunity for an experiment. At the time of our evaluation commission, the federal parliament was discussing the possible creation of a professional, scientific evaluation service; working with a scientific team means gaining experience. This parliamentary service has meanwhile been institutionalized.

The first lesson to be learned from our evaluation is as follows: in cases of IGEs commissioned by political bodies, "entirely new ideas" are not particularly in demand and, indeed, are not seen to be of much use—they are, after all, produced in large quantities by the universities. What is of greater interest is the provision of precise information on the complexity of policies and their implementation. This information must be multidisciplinary, for a Parliamentary Auditing Commission is of necessity interested in several dimensions—legal, procedural, organizational, and so on. Moreover, it is also interested in insights which can, if necessary, be presented in parliament. From this perspective, only the best is good enough. We also suspect that the members of the Auditing Commission were keen to use professional experts (insiders) who could be sent down to the next "rung" in the federal system, that is, the cantons, without shame or loss of face. Thus, it is considered essential that the evaluators should be insiders.

Whether it is actually essential or not, it is impossible for the experts not to look like learners who are putting together a step-by-step account, and who will have to go back to their commissioners again and again to readapt the evaluation structure they devised together. Thus, the second lesson of our evaluation would indicate that experts will always appear to be learners, even if they are insiders:

- Irrespective of their previous experience, they must be open to the unexpected.
- They must avoid the application of simple models and the generalized treatment of all actors.
- Such an approach is clearly not suited to a federal system with twenty-six executive cantons.
- They must be independent and at the same time realize there are only two types of evaluations: those that are politically important and, therefore, quite sensitive, and those that are merely trifling. It is part of the experts' job to work out the political contexts and the consequences of the evaluation.
- Openness, being aware of the complexities and interpreting the political contexts are a condition *sine qua non* for Swiss evaluators. Switzerland is a small country where everybody knows everybody else. Gross errors could mean the end of a person's activity as an evaluator, or even of his or her career.
- Openness and the willingness to assume a learning attitude is particularly important in the case of an IGE evaluation (as well as in federal systems). The lucky cases whereby an expert is appointed by a government or the federal system as a whole are quite rare. The evaluator, therefore, depends on the goodwill and expertise of numerous actors on different executive levels representing different sectorial policies.
- Finally, learning is also an essential part of interaction. The evaluator cannot avoid coming back to his commissioners again and again to readapt the evaluation structure they previously defined together.

In conclusion, therefore, on the basis of our experience and reasoning, there are many reasons why the evaluator should adopt a learning attitude.

A third lesson: the evaluator is influenced by his clients. Their initial questions must be taken seriously and interactive learning always involves reciprocal influence. The commissioners' questions must be given a more precise formulation, dissected into sub-questions and complemented. Some questions will have to be omitted and the evaluator must explain to the commissioners the implications of the question in relation to the methodology and the available data. The same applies to the evaluator's questions. Working together to define the important questions serves to stabilize the expectations of all participants and to create something of a common culture. Our third lesson implies that a stable, common culture must be created by means of interaction. This is all the more important in political contexts as politics are of necessity volatile.

From an evaluator's point of view, political questions must not be confused with scientific hypotheses. This is our fourth lesson. Hypotheses help to stabilize expectations, but, more significantly, they serve to create transparency. The political client and his or her questions do not replace the scientific concept which guides the evaluation. The questions are often linked to specific political contexts and can be subject to constant adjustment by the client in accordance with political popularity and opportunities. Such volatility is not conducive to scientific activity and evaluation which need stability, tranquillity, and peaceful seclusion. Volatility may also result in a (partial) change of the system of reference: new notions may be introduced and new questions raised which do not necessarily coincide with those agreed upon. The danger of confusion is a threat to all IGEs. Hypotheses serve scientific purposes and create transparency for all involved, for the choice of concepts is always a choice of a scientific strategy. The same holds good for the methods. They create transparency and guarantee intersubjectivity. The selection and mastery of these methods is the job of the evaluator, but it is also his job to explain the methods and their limitations to the commissioner. This is a complicated process for both parties. As a common culture of scientific evaluation has not been established between science and politics in Switzerland, it is not possible to develop and use complex scientific models and methods. The fourth lesson claims, therefore, that political questions do not replace a scientific approach.

Our fifth lesson is simple. Due to the combined effects of the extremely complex executive reality arising from the constantly changing conditions and the scientific approach, the evaluation can only be performed in small, iterative steps. This, however, enables the creation of the learning effects which constitute the basis of the evaluation's relevance: it will be taken seriously and be effective. In the course of various evaluations, we have also observed that political commissioners do not like surprises: they see them as the product of strategic behavior. Thus, the gradual, iterative approach is also useful in preventing undesired surprises.

Finally, our sixth lesson concerns responsibility. Even if outsiders evaluate (first lesson), even if they do it by means of being open and of interactive learning (second and third lessons), even if they contribute to transparency by using a scientific approach (fourth lesson) and even if they take an iterative approach (fifth lesson), it is the commissioner or commissioning body that must take ultimate responsibility for the evaluation. This commissioner is democratically elected and authorized to draw conclusions, demand changes and make decisions. The commissioner must, therefore, be involved in crucial decisions. In our case these involved, for instance, the selection of policy areas and cantons and the drawing up of questionnaires. Ultimately it makes sense for the experts to work with variants as this ensures that the politicians chose and decide. This may be contrary to the experts' preferred approach. Nevertheless, they must accept the paradox of democracy whereby the "people are always right." Ultimate responsibility must remain with the politicians.

It is easy to teach such lessons, but can we be sure they are of any value? To answer this question we shall see what happened to our evaluation. The Federal Auditing Commission accepted most of our recommendations. In two instances, however, where our recommendations involved other ministries besides the Ministry of the Interior, of which the FOEP is a part, the commission asked us to work on alternative proposals.

The evaluation has shown that the combination of two federal agencies has not resulted in the establishment of a higher organizational unit but only in the FOEP. In this case, the federal government did not exceed its mandate; it had and still has the right to organize the FOEP as it wishes. The status of the Auditing Commission's findings is merely that of recommendations; in no way do they constitute an imperative for the government. All those involved in the evaluation waited impatiently for the government's response; the government was obliged to inform parliament as to why the recommendations had not been implemented.

The answer took almost two years. The former director of the FOEP has been replaced. He had reached the age of early retirement and agreed to serve his minister as part-time commissioner; his decision to retire was in no way related to the evaluation. The new director had more important things to do than to reorganize his office. He did not avail of offers from the experts to discuss their findings with him. However, the evaluators managed to obtain some information to the effect that the FOEP had indeed started to work on the development of strategic papers, as had been suggested.

The long-awaited answer from the government finally arrived (1994) and came as something of a surprise. Many of the suggestions made by the evaluators and accepted by the Auditing Commission have also been accepted by the government:

- reduce the directorate;
- reduce one level of hierarchy;
- introduce a matrix form of organization; and
- introduce task forces within the FOEP and between ministries and offices at national level; enhance their mode of cooperation in order to avoid conflicting outputs. This measure combined with strategic papers will certainly help the cantons; they will then know what direction to take in accordance with federal strategy and there should be a reduction in contradictory federal statements and advice.

The government did not follow the recommendations of the experts and of the Auditing Commission in the two cases mentioned above which involved other ministries. Here the government argues that switching sections would destroy the existing networks and traditions; this argument is quite valid as the networks referred to involve not only the cantons but also the local authorities.

In our study we evaluated the FOEP in the light of its administrative output and thus of its policy execution. For this reason only certain aspects of environmental policy were broached. For example, the question of the optimal nature of the policy was not examined. This would possibly have brought different facts to light. Note that in policy-oriented evaluation, the style of decision-making should also in principle be taken into account. Under certain circumstances within a federal system, this can lead to what F.W. Scharpf (1988) calls the "joint decision trap." The historical tendency of federal systems to reach decisions through the unanimity rule is not exactly optimal in terms of policy outcome. The models developed by the professionalized segments are often unanimously accepted and implemented by the relevant governments. As in the case of the above mentioned evaluation, the question arising for governments is why they should threaten an existing cemented compromise. Such joint programs are allegedly inefficient, inflexible, unnecessary and somewhat undemocratic.

These programs are inefficient because, comparatively speaking, they are too expensive due to the participation of several levels; in other words there is a tendency to overspend. They are too inflexible because mostly poor and rich areas (in the case of the Federal Republic of Germany) profit from the program, or in other words allocation is not really effective. They are unnecessary in many instances because many important aims have already been attained through federal involvement. Finally, they are often undemocratic because the parliament is often confronted with faits accomplis agreed bureaucratically by the two levels. It would have been a very interesting challenge for us to continue our evaluation along these lines.

Notes

1. These paragraphs are based on U. Kloeti (Kloeti, 1987).
2. The members are not instructed by the cantons on how to vote.
3. While the size of the communes can vary considerably, each commune has just one administration, one parliament, and so on.
4. An outline of the history of Swiss federalism is provided by Knapp (Knapp, 1986)
5. The number of non-technical, unsubstantiated reports and decisions was much lower than we expected. We were unable to judge the necessity and adequacy of the technical standards, calculations and formulas; the commissioners, once informed of this shortcoming, accepted it. It was not, therefore, possible to evaluate the extensive technical output.

References

Kloeti, U. (1987). *Swiss Democracy—Exception or Model?* Zurich: Forschungsstelle für Politische Wissenschaft, University of Zurich.

Knapp, B. (1986). "Etapes du fédéralisme suisse." In *Manuel Système politique de la Suisse*, vol. 3, Berne.

Scharpf, F.W. (1988). "The Joint Decision Trap: Lessons from German Federalism and European Integration." *Public Administration*, vol. 66, Autumn 1988, 239–78.

8

Intergovernmental Evaluation: Patterns and Prospects

Olaf Rieper and Jacques Toulemonde

A Rich Diversity of Case Studies

The chapters in this book have documented the huge, overwhelming variety of governmental levels and the heterogeneity of the administrative and political context in more than seven different countries and regions. Some of these variations and heterogeneities are described in the first section of this chapter. The second section poses the question of whether IGEs have any particular problems and challenges that distinguish them from single level evaluations. The third section addresses the special challenges in relation to the use of IGEs. And in the fourth section we seek to summarize the lessons learned.

One variation concerns the general political system in which IGEs operate. These systems include unitary states (Denmark, Sweden, and England), confederal structures (European Union and Switzerland) as well as federal systems (U.S. and Canada) with a variation in size ranging from more than 300 million to 5 million inhabitants. Another variation concerns the different levels of government that are involved in programs subject to IGEs. These include the municipalities and counties of the Scandinavian countries, the European Union and its relations with the European Member States, and the states of the U.S. in relation to the federal governmental level. A third variation can be found in the kind of program. These programs belong to different sectors of the societies concerned and include personal services (education, social work, health) the labor market (employment and training), legal aid, regional development, science and technology, merger control, and environmental conservation.

The heterogeneity springs from the approaches adopted by the authors. One aspect concerns the roles of the authors vis-à-vis their subject. In some chapters the author plays the role of an evaluator (Denmark and Switzerland), and in others the author is more of an observer, viewing the progress of the IGEs from a distance (Canada, U.S., European Union, Great Britain, and Sweden). We must also remember that the authors come from different institutional bodies ranging from governmental agencies and research centers to universities.

The authors' heterogeneity is also reflected in the characteristic contents of their respective chapters. In the chapters about Denmark, Switzerland, and Canada, cases of IGE are described in some detail. However, in other chapters, U.S. and England, the level of description is more general, offering descriptions of evaluative institutions involved in IGE and giving examples of IGEs, though these are not in-depth case-studies. The high degree of heterogeneity implies that comparison in a strict sense, variable for variable, is not possible. Instead, the heterogeneity provides a rich source of inspiration as to what hypotheses and issues should be dealt with in IGE.

Every chapter provides at least one example of evaluation that potentially involves several levels of government. Some chapters present several detailed cases: three in the European Union and two in Canada. This makes ten examples ranked according to their intergovernmental profile; they range from evaluations conducted by a single level of government or less, in some cases, and finally, evaluations undertaken separately by two competing levels.

Governments Evaluate Together in Partnership

Two cases dealt with the European regional development programs and closely matched our definition of intergovernmental evaluation. The main area authorities were a Danish county (Rieper) and the Republic of Ireland (Toulemonde). In both cases intergovernmental relations were mainly bilateral: programs were specific to the areas, decisions to evaluate were negotiated in accordance with the agendas of both levels, and evaluation questions were specially worded by representatives of both levels for the programs in question.

Both examples had an almost complete intergovernmental profile in the sense that interaction between the area authorities and the upper levels took place at various stages of the evaluation process. Both evaluations were performed by a research institution highly credible with all relevant levels of government. Both were selected and permanently steered by a monitoring committee with representatives from several levels of government. In both cases, authorities at different levels used the results for their own purposes. Of the situations described in this book, these two cases seem to be the most typically intergovernmental. Thus it is worth examining in more depth the extent to which the two stories can be qualified as useful evaluations.

When the time comes to define and word evaluation questions, one would imagine that different levels of government would express their own concerns and that the evaluation would proceed by adding together all the issues that were relevant or critical at a given period of time. In fact, in the Danish and Irish examples, some sensitive potential problems did not surface at all, but were excluded by organizational means or by narrowing the topics for evaluation. In the Irish case, a critical evaluation question dealt with ways of creating jobs: the European authorities favored indigenous development in the country while the national government also wanted to attract inward investments. In fact, this controversial question was prevented from appearing on the evaluation agenda.

In the Danish case, the evaluation questions were mainly directed towards the county and focused on intermediary goals such as the enhanced use of computers and the qualifications of employees in regional SMEs, thus making the findings less relevant for the national and the European level. This was accepted by the representatives of these levels of government who admitted that evaluation was primarily relevant for the counties. If all the upper levels of government had had a vested interest in the evaluation, it would have been difficult to negotiate the very disparate evaluation criteria and to agree on a single evaluation design.

Both cases show that by shaping the evaluation focus within the predefined and accepted political climate surrounding the programs, sensitive political problems are kept out of IGEs. This can be explained by a feature of European regional development programs whose design, planning, and implementation create a high degree of consensus among the governments involved. This consensus should not be threatened by evaluation and the participating actors are selected to avoid confrontation. As for the evaluators, they accept self-censorship more or less conscientiously, or accept the restricted list of evaluation questions which survives the early stages of the negotiations.

Governments Evaluate Together, with One in Command

In Canada, federal and provincial governments interacted in the evaluation of legal aid programs initiated at the upper level and implemented by the ten provinces under a federal/provincial cost-sharing agreement (Segsworth and Poel). This evaluation was dominated by the federal level at all stages. The design of the policy and its evaluation was multilateral in the sense that the upper level dominated the process and unified almost everything across the country. For example, it imposed time schedules, paid evaluators, formulated the questions to be dealt with, and chose evaluators and methods.

However, the provinces negotiated some aspects of the evaluation design and took part in some of the research work. Involvement of the lower level authorities was especially significant in the case of Ontario, the biggest Canadian province, which played a more important role than the others in both the program and its evaluation. Thanks to its financial and political weight, the province of Ontario gave a more bilateral shape to intergovernmental relations. Finally, in this case, the evaluation profile was almost completely intergovernmental, except that both levels took little notice of the evaluation findings. In addition, the provincial government pressed ahead with major policy and program concerns that had been excluded from the evaluation design.

The next case comes from Switzerland where an environmental conservation agency was evaluated on the initiative of the confederal parliament (Zimmermann and Knoepfel). From the very beginning, this evaluation was instigated and managed by the confederal level, which focused the work on organizational matters and on administrative output rather than on policy effectiveness. The evaluation work was entrusted to a neutral research body whose task was to judge the ability of the agency to implement environmental policies. This was done by means of an implementation analysis and through a survey across actors at confederal and cantonal levels. The cantons played a very small part in politically sensitive choices and direct interaction between levels was buffered by the intermediary function of evaluators. Finally, the evaluation did not threaten the professional consensus of the confederal and cantonal actors belonging to the environmental policy network. The most critical information dealt with interpolicy choices (e.g., environment versus transport) rather than with intergovernmental choices (confederation versus cantons).

One Government Evaluates for the Sake of Another

In the chapters about the Swedish school system and about the evaluative institutions in England concerning personal social services, the evaluation mechanisms operate on a continuous basis, and not ad hoc as in the previous cases of IGEs on specific programs. These institutions work in a intergovernmental political context but the political legitimacy of their mandate rests with one government level. However, in both countries the evaluations are conducted in a more intergovernmental manner than might be expected judging by their formal operational structure.

The Swedish school system has recently been changed, increasing its autonomy in relation to the local government and the school directors and teachers. Furubo describes how the national agency previously controlling and monitoring the school system by inspection, regulation, and surveillance, has been transformed into an evaluation body that produces follow-up and evaluation information, used by the actors in the school system at the local level. The information aims at helping the politicians at the local level as well as the professionals in the school system to make comparisons, give them food for thought and stimulate personal reflections and judgments. However, the evaluations are in the hands of an agency with major control of the evaluation process at the national level.

Despite the imbalance between a decentralized school system with a high degree of autonomy vis-à-vis the local government and an evaluation agency which is part of the national government, the conflict between the two levels of government has not arisen. According to Furubo, one explanation for this relative harmony is the corporative nature of the Swedish school system with powerful professionals, pressure groups of users (parents), and civil servants demanding the same kind of information for the same purpose—that purpose being the incremental development of the school system, not a fundamental reform in any sense. One might expect a high amount of informal communication between different levels of government in such a system. One might also regard the corporative characteristic of the school policy as an element of the Swedish welfare system itself. A supplementary explanation is afforded in the fact that many local governments are small and lack sufficient evaluative capacity. They are therefore unable to formulate alternative evaluative criteria or designs.

Unlike Sweden, England has seen a tendency towards centralization in the last decade. The power of local government to raise revenue and determine how it will spend its financial resources has been reduced and the leadership of the national government has been extended. Against that intergovernmental background, Henkel gives a number of examples of IGE within the social services. IGE involving central and local government is most apparent in the work of evaluative institutions established by government for monitoring and evaluating the performance of local government: inspectorates and the Audit Commission. In the beginning of the 1990s, evaluation changed direction from emphasis on economy to quality criteria in public services. There was a shift towards encouragement of internal evaluation mechanisms, especially internal performance review, and quality assurance systems. Along with these changes came a broadening of the concept of accountability, a focus on standards, measures and performance indicators as means by which the public could judge public services and make informed choices.

The Social Services Inspectorate and the Audit Commission belong to the national level government, but operating agencies and service users are involved in consultative procedures between central and local government. Networking and consultation are increasingly obvious in their evaluative processes. However, these evaluation institutions provide examples of unbalanced versions of IGE. They incorporate members from other tiers in their teams and consult with them on the investigation agenda, but the agenda belongs to the center. The two key evaluation institutions are based at the national level, but interact with lower levels throughout the evaluation process. There seems to be a combination of formal consultation and informal networking across levels of government.

The impact of the European Science and Technology policy in France (Toulemonde) illustrates the evaluations that were carried out by a government for use by policymakers at another level. A large survey was launched by the European Union to find out whether European programs had modified French national R&D strategies. The evaluation was entrusted to a team led by a highly regarded French academic research center which consulted the French scientific community on a broad base. As in the former case, informal consultation and networking greatly contributed to the credibility of the findings, although the evaluations never openly appeared as intergovernmental.

In this case, the most politically sensitive question was that of subsidarity: which level, either the national government or the European government, is the most effective in the field of R&D policies? Such a risky question was not totally overlooked in the evaluation process, as might be expected if one looks at the previous examples. The evaluation report indirectly addressed the problem by referring to duplication/complementarity between national and European programs. Although this evaluation was given the green light, funded and monitored at the European level, its sole addressee was the French government which would receive the evaluation report just when it assumed the presidency of the European Council.

Governments Avoid Interaction

One of the Canadian examples (EOP) illustrates a total absence of interaction in the evaluation of a program which, in many ways, would have been an ideal candidate for intergovernmental evaluation as it involved the transfer of federal funds to provinces and the implementation of a federal policy by provinces and municipalities. The purpose of this particular program was to help unemployed people return to work. The evaluation was totally in the hands of the provincial department in charge of the program. Interaction with federal departments was deliberately avoided, so that questions about potential overlapping or incompatibilities between levels of government were systematically put aside.

The evaluation report stated that parts of the program were largely ineffective. The evaluators might not have been allowed to express such a clear-cut judgment in a more intergovernmental environment. However, the conclusive nature of the evaluation work did not result in the efficient use of its findings. This was clearly due to the lack of publicity given to the debates on the program which were limited to a small administrative circle and consequently easily forgotten when key actors moved to other posts.

Governments Compete Through Evaluation

The difficult relations that prevail when levels of government are in competition also surface in evaluation. This conflicting situation was exemplified by the case of the Second European Framework Program for R&D (Toulemonde). Two national governments, the United Kingdom and the Netherlands, took advantage of their temporary presidency of the European Council to launch a counter evaluation that replicated that of the Commission. They entrusted the study to a well-known British research center which made a broad survey of national representatives.

To a large extent, the two national governments wanted to ensure that the evaluation would be sensitive to national level issues, although it had already been evaluated for the European level. However, the conclusions of this counter evaluation did not differ much from those already obtained by the Commission. The Council's attempts to judge for itself by itself were impeded by its lack of evaluation resources and capacities.

Finally, evaluation does not appear to be a dangerous weapon in the hands of governments who fight against on another. This has been suggested by Derlien (1989) who tells the story of the German Federal Government launching experiments in the field of education, which is constitutionally the task of the *Länder* level. This operation gave birth to one of the main evaluation streams in Germany. It seems that the *Länder* did not even feel the need to react by launching counter evaluations. The federal weapon was simply weakened by putting the evaluation results at a high degree of politization.

In the introductory chapter, IGE was defined as the interaction of at least two levels of government at one stage or more of the evaluation process, these stages starting from the decision to evaluate and ending in the utilization of results. In the literature we reviewed, the IGE theme has received very little attention from professionals and scholars alike. We feel that this poor state of theory and practice reflects specific difficulties related to IGE and is by no means an excuse for lack of interest in the subject. On the contrary, sharing in evaluation across levels of government raises a series of challenging questions which must be and can be answered.

IGEs Differ Significantly from Single Level Evaluations

A basic question is whether IGEs have specific characteristics, or whether they are fully contingent upon the administrative/political environments in which they operate. It is not surprising that this question is examined here, since this book would be of no interest if the answer were in the negative. The specificities of an IGE can be sought either in its organizational aspect or in its political dimension.

IGE makes it possible to compare the performances of area authorities, provided it is organized in a multilateral way, that is to say involving the upper level and all governments at the lower level. This possibility is fully exploited by the Swedish National Agency for Education (Furubo) and in the "national program of special studies" undertaken by the British Audit Commission (Henkel). This possibility materialized in a special way when the U.S. federal administration used an evaluation by the Californian government as an example for other states (Morra).

Such worthwhile possibilities represent the pros of IGE. The cons on the other hand are the organizational difficulties that cannot be avoided when governments of different levels interact. It is difficult enough to make the evaluation process fit a political agenda when a single government is concerned. This difficulty is multiplied when new authorities enter the arena and is clearly exemplified by the case of the Ontario Legal Aid Plan. This evaluation arrived late and was based on an incomplete research agenda, given the new policy and program interests of a new provincial government (Segsworth and Poel). Another obvious difficulty emerges from the Danish evaluation of a regional development program (Rieper): the more numerous the levels of government involved in the evaluation process, the more varied the goals, objectives and questions with which the evaluation must deal. If the terms of reference were established by adding up the interests of each level, exercise management would soon be impossible.

However, although these organizational features may be important, one could easily find similar characteristics in multisite evaluations where the program under evaluation is implemented by several institutions that are not governments. Consequently, we believe that these organizational specificities are not sufficient to typify IGEs, and that one should look at more political ingredients.

Within different political regimes and different public sectors, there is a tendency to organize, design, and focus evaluations which are unlikely to threaten the legitimacy of different levels of government. This is apparently done by consulting key people at every level, often in an informal way, by censoring questions of too sensitive a nature, by gathering and analyzing data which match the needs of different governments and by choosing evaluators whom everybody considers highly credible. Looking at these IGE features, we find obvious similarities with single level evaluations if one reads "stakeholders" for "level of government." In fact, these conclusions come very close to those of Rist (1993) who finds successful organizational learning when the evaluation process relies on informal contacts and strategies of "no surprises." However these features are more pronounced in an IGE because each level has to defend its political legitimacy. Evaluations are usually not allowed to jeopardize that legitimacy in any way.

Thus, the specificity of any IGE is mainly a question of degree: they contain a larger share of the political ingredients than other types of evaluation. Nevertheless, one of our examples suggests that there is a specificity of nature and not only one of degree. The joint evaluation of the European regional development program in Ireland (Toulemonde) failed to address a critical problem for a reason which only exists in intergovernmental relations: that of evaluating the best way to create jobs, implying a balance between the development of local enterprises and inward investment. Both European and national levels of government are equipped to create their own balance between these two objectives. Both enjoy an undisputed legitimacy to decide for themselves and this results in significantly different judgments: Brussels favors indigenous development much more than Dublin. In single government evaluations, it is normal for opposite views to be expressed about public interest questions but only one authority has the political legitimacy to reach a definitive decision. In intergovernmental contexts, there are not only different legitimate conceptions of what is in the public interest, but also different legitimate arenas where these conceptions are submitted to arbitration.

Before leaving the question of the specificities of IGEs, we must point out the trap which would consist in qualifying as an IGE any evaluation involving civil servants who belong to public authorities at different levels. In several of the previous cases, and especially in the evaluation of the Swiss Environmental Agency (Zimmermann and Knoepfel) it appears that people represent their professional community or their policy network rather than their level of government.

IGEs Remain Similar Whatever Their Altitude Above Street Level

This issues is critical since it had been assumed that constant problems appeared but differed, depending on whether interacting governments were close to the "ground" or to the "sky." In fact, the previous section shows that the characteristics of IGEs have been taken from almost all our chapters, regardless of whether they deal with powerful institutions like the U.S. federal government or the European Commission or with tiny authorities like Swedish municipalities or Swiss cantons.

Nevertheless, some facts contradict our assumption. In the U.S., it is recognized that evaluations at the state level have generally poorer technical standards than those at the federal level (Morra). For example small area authorities are often unable to build up the large samples that statistical validity would require. This makes it difficult to satisfy both levels with a single IGE and, in fact, few intergovernmental features can be found in American evaluations. It is worth noting that the case which best fits our definition of IGE involves California, a large, powerful state whose government might be considered closer to the "sky" than to the "ground."

Thus, the small size of area authorities at the lowest levels poses special technical problems to evaluators which they do not encounter at higher levels.

However, the assumption that there are constant characteristics throughout IGEs is borne out by the evaluation of the Danish regional development program (Rieper). This evaluation includes both the "sky" (European Union) and the "ground" (Danish municipalities) and all the intermediary levels. All levels were involved in the evaluation process and the qualitative methodology that was used provided fuel for instrumental and conceptual utilization at all levels. In this case, specific features of IGEs apply equally to all levels: opportunities for comparing areas at the lower level, heterogeneity of goals across levels, conflicts of legitimacy and absence of ultimate political arbitration.

Interaction Is Unavoidable

At the beginning of this book we stressed the paradoxical nature of having many intergovernmental programs and policies but having few descriptions of evaluations that, by being IGEs, match the intergovernmental character of the programs. The different chapters of this book confirm this paradox. It is surprising that few of the IGEs presented in this book are fully fledged, in the sense that interaction between levels of government occurs at almost every stage of the evaluation process, and not just at one stage. At the same time, almost all the programs or policies which have been mentioned so far are partly financed or co-run by several levels of government. Although our collective work has constantly focused on IGEs, the paradoxical imbalance that was observed in the literature still remains and is even accentuated by what we have learned.

Interactions between governments are patently difficult exercises, especially in the sensitive situations that crop up during evaluation. Thus one might suggest evaluating the growing number of intergovernmental programs in a parallel way, each authority conducting its own study and avoiding interaction with other levels. Our previous chapters clearly show the risks of adopting such a strategy. The first drawback is that of limiting the evaluation process to a small circle and then preventing the level of government which is kept out of the circle from taking an interest in the evaluation findings. In the case of intergovernmental programs, this leads directly to a total absence of utilization as was the case for the Employment Opportunity Program in Canada (Segsworth and Poel).

The second risk is that of costly, unproductive duplication as was the case in the evaluation of the European Framework Program for R&D (Toulemonde). There is no serious evaluation without field data gathering, a stage which proved to be a bottleneck in the European example. The counter evaluation, which was launched by the national level of government at the national level, did not manage to duplicate the field data collection already effected by the European level. This seriously weakened the counter evaluation. If duplication of the surveys and questionnaires had been decided, a new, even more critical problem would have appeared: that of presenting the beneficiaries and citizens with a woolly, confusing image of public management.

Bearing the previous chapter in mind, we infer that intergovernmental evaluations cannot avoid interaction, at least at one or two stages. If this point is not contradicted by further research and debates, it raises serious concerns about seeing so much interaction in policies and programs and so little in evaluations.

Is Interaction Always Useful?

In the Introduction we proposed a preliminary explanation for this imbalance by saying that not all intergovernmental programs deserve to be evaluated with the same emphasis on interaction. We assumed that, apart from technical and organizational difficulties, which are inherent to IGEs, one should choose to make governments interact strongly or weakly according to the way in which the evaluation will be used. Three basic models of utilization were presented as follow:

Managerial model. This type of utilization implies that evaluation findings are fed back into the program management in an instrumental way in order to improve or redirect objectives, means or procedures. We assumed that managerial use of IGEs is restricted by pragmatic constraints which lessen the value of information produced.

Democratic model. This model puts the emphasis on the accountability of the different levels of government. We assumed that this model under threat from potential political conflicts involving legitimacy.

Conceptual model. In this case, the evaluation process helps actors at different levels to develop a common understanding of effects and judgment criteria. We assumed that this type of IGE could become part of a broad societal learning system in which evaluation deals with questions that all the levels of government involved feel free to discuss.

In the following section, we confront these assumptions with the facts appearing in our different chapters.

The Closer the Interaction, the More Useful the Evaluation

Before going through the cases in this book to see whether the difficult question of utilization can be answered or rephrased, some self-criticism is needed. In none of the cases has the utilization of the IGEs been studied in its own right. Most of the statements about utilization are based on the authors' experience, interviews and readings about the actual cases. Therefore the evidence of use is somehow fragile. Nevertheless, the authors were close to their cases, and their experience and judgment are thought to be adequate for the main tendencies, even if not fully correct in details.

At first, this section must omit the cases in which the authors found no evidence of utilization: these are the two Canadian cases. (The evaluation of the Ontario Legal Aid Plan might have been put to better use if the provincial government in office at the conclusion of the study been in power at the outset, i.e. had participated in the evaluation design.) The conflicting evaluation of the European Framework Program for R&D must also be put aside since the kind of negative interaction which occurred in this case seems to have added no value to the policymaking process.

Only two of the previous chapters provide examples that support our assumptions. The Swiss evaluation of environmental conservation policy is a case of weak interaction where the confederal level is clearly dominant. This case indicates instrumental use by middle management personnel at confederal level. Another example is the study of the impact of European research programs on the French scientific milieu. This study was entirely initiated and controlled by Brussels with the obvious intention of accounting to the Member States. In both cases evaluations had a low intergovernmental profile and were used for management or democratic purposes by the level of government which took the leadership. This concurs with our assumption that strong interaction complicates instrumental feedback and raises political risks when governments account to their respective electorates.

Nevertheless, our assumptions are contradicted in the five remaining cases as is shown below. Although the exploratory nature of our work must be kept in mind, the contradiction between our assumptions and the facts leads us to describe the art of organizing useful interaction in a different way. We can no longer assume that IGEs are only good at providing food for thought or at pointing to some conceptual utilization, which was our hypothesis in the introductory chapter. This book suggests a simpler conception which may be worded as follow: *in cases of joint policies and programs, the most useful evaluations are those which involve the closest interactions between levels of government.*

A typical example is that of the evaluation of the European regional development program in Ireland. The evaluation process was entirely interactive and the report was discussed by a committee including representatives from both levels of government. The results was discussed in special seminars in Brussels and in Dublin. The conclusions were utilized by the Irish government during negotiations for the Treaty of Maastricht. In Brussels the European Commission used the report to justify the rationale behind its regional policy and to argue for an increase in European aid to backward regions in the member states. In this case three utilization models were reported at the European level as well as at national level in Ireland. Although some sensitive questions seem to have been censored, this example shows a very close interaction and a wide range of utilizations.

In Sweden, in the school sector, a national agency is continuously performing IGEs which are used conceptually as well as instrumentally by the local and the national level, and often in some interaction between the two levels of government. This is also the case of the United Kingdom, where the IGEs of the Audit Commission and Social Service Inspectorates are used in a highly structured way by local governments and agencies, often in interaction with agents at the national level. This use seems to be managerial for the most part but some kind of accountability also seems to be at stake. In these instances our assumption concerning the pragmatic constraints of managerial uses is negated. This might be due to the way the evaluation institutions and mechanisms are build into the political-administrative context of both countries, making the reporting and disseminating procedures well known and facilitating access to information by the potential users. Conceptual use is also reported in Sweden in relation to the professional consensus which prevails in the school system. These two examples indicate that similar kinds of multilateral interaction can lead to significant utilization.

The Danish evaluation is another example dealing with European regional policy. It was also organized in an intergovernmental way from first to last but the results were not used as much as in the Irish case. This was probably due to the fact that, although many meetings enabled interaction to take place, European and national levels implicitly decided not to interact and to leave the entire responsibility for the work to the county. In the end, the evaluation focused mainly on regional needs for information about short-term benefits from the program, a question that was not at the top of European and national agendas. Although this example involves considerable formal interaction, it could be described as being in reality a case of weak interaction and limited utilization.

In the case of the youth employment program in America, there was a managerial use of evaluation at different levels of different governments. Information produced by the Californian study was used by the federal administration as feedback to the policymaking process in other states. However, the evaluation was totally controlled by Californian authorities except at the very last stage of utilization. We think that this case is one of weak interaction, where utilization stemmed from a happy accident rather than from the IGE's intrinsic potentialities.

The Necessary Art of Inducing Governments to Interact

A still more complex pattern of interaction, cooperation, joint responsibilities and cost-sharing between levels of government is emerging. This is true on a small scale between national governments, regional authorities and municipalities as well as on a large scale between states and the federal and confederal level.

In conclusion, we feel entitled to assume that these joint policies and programs should be evaluated with as much interaction as possible between levels of government. It must also be admitted that high intergovernmental profiles are rare, if not exceptional.

Finally, there is a need to induce governments to interact more in evaluation processes and to seriously improve the current situation. The various chapters point to a series of problems which will have to be dealt with by those engaged in this work:

- interaction may be extended to the whole evaluation process or to one or several stages only;
- evaluation may involve a partnership between equally powerful levels or leadership of one government;
- interaction may be bilateral (limited to one area authority at the lower level), or multilateral (extended to the whole territory of the upper level);
- interaction may be organized formally and/or informally;
- the list of questions to be dealt with may be expanded by including the concerns of different governments or may be reduced by the removal of conflicting issues;
- the joint research work may be limited to data collection only, or may be extended to common analysis and joint conclusions; and
- the evaluation may be commissioned by an institution which has close links with both levels of government or is seen to be independent by both parties.

These problems are obviously difficult to solve, especially in view of the fact that they are closely interconnected. However, we cannot end this book without making a loud worldwide call for their resolution. We feel that obscure, changing intergovernmental relations are like ominous clouds that darken the political skies over our democracies and will provoke a lack of confidence among citizens if nothing is done to shed light on the matter. Intergovernmental evaluation is therefore much more than a relevant subject of study, it is indeed an urgent social duty.

Contributors

JAN ERIC FURUBO is the head of the Division for Results Based Management, Evaluation, and Budgetary Questions in the National Audit Bureau of Sweden and the author of books and articles in the fields of evaluation and budgeting. A central focus of this writings has been the study of the effects of information campaigns and other policy instruments in areas such as energy conservation and health policy. He has recently been appointed secretary general of the European Evaluation Society.

MARY HENKEL is a senior lecturer in the Department of Government, Brunel University, UK and a member of the Centre for the Evaluation of Public Policy and Practice at Brunnel. She has done extensive research on public sector evaluative institutions and quality policies in the UK. She is currently the UK director of a three country study of higher education reforms. Her publications include *Government, Evaluation and Change*, Jessica Kingsley Publications, 1991.

PETER KNOEPFEL (Dr. phil University of Bern in 1977) was project director and senior research fellow at the Scientific Centre for Social Sciences in Berlin (WZB ; 1977-1982). Since then is a professor for public policy analysis and environmental policies at the Institute for Advanced Studies in public administration (Institut de Hautes Etudes en Administration Publique—IDHEAP), where in 1994 he was appointed director. He has been involved in many research activities such as: public policy analysis, environmental policies, air quality policies. He is also president of the Swiss Commission for the observation of the environment of the Swiss Academy of Natural Sciences.

LINDA G. MORRA is director of Education and Employment Issues for the U.S. General Accounting Office. Within the GAO, Ms. Morra has also directed Intergovernmental and Management Issues and the Congressional Request Group. She was deputy to the director of GAO's

Office of Program Planning after having worked in its Program Evaluation and Methodology Division. Ms. Morra has received several GAO awards, including GAO's Distinguished Service Award, and its active in the American Evaluation and American Education Research Associations. Ms. Morra did her doctorate in educational evaluation and research at the University of Virginia.

DALE H. POEL (Ph. D. Iowa) is a professor at the School of Public Administration in Dalhousic University's Faculty of Management. He is a specialist in applied research and teaches program evaluation in the MPA program. He has conducted evaluation research for Justice Canada, the Solicitor General Canada, the Nova Scotia Commission on Drug Dependency, the City of Halifax, the New Brunswick Department of Justice, the Nova Scotia Legal Aid Commission, the Canadian Mental Health Association/Nova Scotia Division and Health and Welfare Canada. He was a Senior Research Associate with the Nova Scotia Royal Commission on Health Care. His current research includes a pilot project in judicial evaluation for the province of Nova Scotia and the development, with a national research team, of participatory models of evaluation for the Canadian healthy communities initiatives.

OLAF RIEPER has an MA in sociology (1974) and a PhD in Organisation Theory from the Copenhagen School of Economics and Social Sciences (1984), and is a senior researcher at the Danish Local Government Research Institute (AKF), Copenhagen, since 1985. Prior to that he was an associate professor at the Copenhagen School of Economics and Social Sciences, The University of Copenhagen, the Danish Institute of Technology, and the University of Michigan. He was awarded first prize for a monograph on Working Environment Year 2000. Mr Rieper is the author of, *"Enterprises and Programmes for Regional Technological Development"*, in Cronberg, T. et al. (eds.): Danish Experiments—Social Constructions of Technology, 1991. He is a member of the working group on "Policy and Programme Evaluation " under the auspices of the IIAS and was a member of a panel of European Experts which recently conducted an audit on evaluation practices within the European Commission.

ROBERT V. SEGSWORTH is Professor of Political Science at Laurential University, Sudbury, Canada. He is the editor of *The Canadian Journal of Program Evaluation.* He has co-edited *Budgeting, Auditing and Evaluation: Functions and integration in Seven Governments* with Andrew Gray and Bill Jenkins and has published articles in such journals as *Knowledge and Society, The International Review of Administrative Science* and *Canadian Public Administration.* Current research includes work on *The New Public Management, Auditing and Accountability* and *Policy Convergence: Auditing and Evaluation in the Canadian Provinces.*

JACQUES TOULEMONDE teaches economics at the "Ecole Nationale des Travaux Publics de l'Etat" in Lyon, France. He is a co-founder of the Centre for European Evaluation Expertise, where he co-ordinates a large European programme on Regional Policy evaluation. His publications deal with the evaluation of R & D and Regional Policies. He is a member of the working group on "Policy and Program Evaluation" under the auspices of the IIAS. He was a member of a panel of European Experts which recently conducted an audit on evaluation practices within the European Commission.

WILLI ZIMMERMANN (Dr. phil University of Munich, 1987) studied political science, philosophy, and psychology. His current position is that of senior lecturer and research fellow at Geneva University. Mr. Zimmermann lectures on public administration and policy analysis and is involved in research projects, particularly in the area of implementing environmental protection. He also works extensively in the field of evaluation research and carries out evaluations, focusing both on institutions and policies. He directs a private research company Bern, Switzerland and is currently evaluating the Swiss contribution to the transformation of the labour unions in Rumania, Bulgaria, and the Slovak Republic (1995). Mr. Zimmermann has close links with Prof. Peter Knoepfel and other teaching activities in different European countries.

Index

49, 57, 67, 75, 101; Municipal, 26, 101; County, 26, 101. *See also* Associations of authorities

Partnership, 4, 121, 137, 152; *See also* Interaction

Peer review, 46; *See also* Socio-political system

Performance review, 32, 49; *See also* Evaluation

Policies: competing, 10, 93; separated, 11; overlapping, 11; inclusive, 11; self imposed, 27.

Policy domains: education, 28, 69; research, 16, 124; economic development, 16, 76, 99, 121; social services, 46; employment, 83; justice, 87; environment, 133.

Policy fountain, 9; *See also* Co-operative model

Policy law of gravity, 9; *See also* Cooperative model

Political ingredient, 22, 91; *See also* Evaluation model

Political resources: public arena, 8, 22; checks and balances, 8; taxation power, 8, 43, 101; power to interpret regulation, 30; *See also* Autonomy, Electorate

Political system: government, 8; self government, 26; constituencies, 8; federalism, 12; decentralisation, 13; subsidiarity, 117, 123, 126.

Power distribution, 37; symmetry in, 11, 21; asymmetry in, 41.

Professional community, 4, 36, 155, 160; *See also* Socio-political system

Professionalised segment, 148; *See also* Socio-political system

Shared cost programs, 79; *See also* Intergovernmental

Socio-political system, 135; *See also* Corporatism, Professionalised segment, Professional community, Peer review

Subsidiarity, 117, 123, 126; *See also* Political system

Supervision, 12; *See also* Agent model

Utilisation, 4; instrumental use, 86, 91, 104, 128; symbolic use, 111; conceptual use, 4, 21, 104, 163; understanding use, 94; *See also* Formative evaluation, Learning, Accountability

The International Institute of Administrative Sciences and Its Working Group on Policy and Program Evaluation

The International Institute of Administrative Sciences (IIAS) is a scientific institution, whose vocation is international, specializing in public administration and the administrative sciences. Its field covers all questions which concern contemporary public administration at the national and international levels. Imagined already as early as 1910 by administrators and politicians and established in 1930 by the International Congress of Administrative Sciences held in Madrid, the IIAS is the first of the specialized institutions to affirms, worldwide, its scientific willingness to resolve the problems and challenges of national and international administration.

The purpose of the IIAS is to promote the development of administrative sciences, the better operation of public administrative agencies, the improvement of administrative methods and technics and the progress of international administration. Its history demonstrates its capacity to respond to the needs of the industrialized and developing countries, as well as to those in transition. Owing to its attributes and great experience, the IIAS is a unique organization which is comprised of 48 Member States, 9 Governmental International Organizations, 49 National Sections and 54 Corporate Members.

A large part of IIAS activities is devoted to information (IIAS publications, its quarterly International Review of Administrative Sciences, published in French and English, and its information and documentation service attached to its Library) and to expertise and consultancy. The Institute responds to specific requests of governments, international organizations or any other agency. But most IIAS research activities are carried out in the framework of its annual major meetings (Congress, Conference or Round Table) and its Working Groups (12 currently).

One of these Working Groups, and one of the most productive, was launched in 1986 and, since this date, has been working on Policy and Program Evaluation. Since its beginning, the Dr. Ray C. Rist has presided, the group meets once a year and, in the framework of sub-groups, prepares books which present the findings of their intensive research. The latest book, *Politics and Practices of Intergovernmental Evaluation,* presents the efforts of one of these sub-groups.

IIAS, rue Defacqz 1 box 11, B-1050 BRUXELLES, BELGIQUE